WHEN MACHIAVELLI's brief treatise on Renaissance statecraft and princely power was posthumously printed in 1532, it generated a debate which has raged unabated until the present day. Written in 1513 after Machiavelli's enforced retirement from diplomatic service for the Republic of Florence, *The Prince* provided an analysis of the usually violent means by which men seize, retain, and lose political power. Machiavelli's original treatment of the major philosophical and political questions of his times, especially the relationship between public deeds and private morality, added a dimension of incisive realism to traditional discourse on the nature of the state which, according to Machiavelli, had far too often focused only upon ideal theoretical conditions rather than upon actual political practice.

Niccolò Machiavelli was born in Florence in 1469. Very little is known of his life until his entrance into the Florentine Chancery in 1498, where he served his mentor, the Florentine Standardbearer Piero Soderini, until the return of the Medici in 1512 overthrew Soderini's republic and caused Machiavelli both the loss of his position and even brief imprisonment for his republican sympathies. In addition to a longer and more complicated work on republics, *The Discourses*, Machiavelli wrote *The Art of War*, *The History of Florence*, lyric poetry, a novella, a number of brief essays and diplomatic narratives, and several plays, including the masterpiece of Italian Renaissance comedy, *The Mandrake Root*. He died in 1527.

PETER BONDANELLA, editor and co-translator of this edition, is Professor of Italian at Indiana University, where he teaches Renaissance literature and cinema, and is Director of the Center for Italian Studies. He is the author of *Machiavelli and the Art of Renaissance History*, *Francesco Guicciardini*, and *Italian Cinema: From Neorealism to the Present*; editor of *Federico Fellini: Essays in Criticism*; co-editor of *The Macmillan Dictionary of Italian Literature*; and co-translator of *The Portable Machiavelli* and *The Decameron*.

MARK MUSA, co-translator of this edition, is Distinguished Professor of Italian at Indiana University, where he teaches Medieval literature. He is the author of *Essays on Dante*, and *Advent at the Gates: Dante's Comedy*, and has translated Dante's *Vita Nuova* and *The Divine Comedy*; he is the co-translator of *The Portable Machiavelli* and *The Decameron*.

THE WORLD'S CLASSICS

NICCOLÒ MACHIAVELLI

The Prince

Edited with an Introduction by
PETER BONDANELLA

Translated by
PETER BONDANELLA
and
MARK MUSA

Oxford   New York
OXFORD UNIVERSITY PRESS

Oxford University Press, Walton Street, Oxford OX2 6DP

Oxford New York Toronto
Delhi Bombay Calcutta Madras Karachi
Petaling Jaya Singapore Hong Kong Tokyo
Nairobi Dar es Salaam Cape Town
Melbourne Auckland

and associated companies in
Berlin Ibadan

Oxford is a trade mark of Oxford University Press

British Library Cataloguing in Publication Data

Machiavelli, Niccolò
Il Principe.—(The world's classics)
1. State, The   2. Political science—Early works to 1700
3. Political ethic
I. Title   II. Bondanella, Peter
III. Musa, Mark
320. 1'01   JC11

ISBN 0-19-281602-0

Library of Congress Cataloging in Publication Data

Machiavelli, Niccolò, 1469-1527.
The prince.
(The World's classics)
Translation of: Il Principe.
Bibliography: p.
1. Political science—Early works to 1700.
2. Political ethics. I. Bondanella, Peter E. 1943
II. Title.
JC143.M38   1984   320.1   81-13059

ISBN 0-19-281602-0 (pbk.)

Printed in Great Britain by
BPCC Hazell Books
Aylesbury, Bucks.

CONTENTS

CONTENTS

THE PRINCE

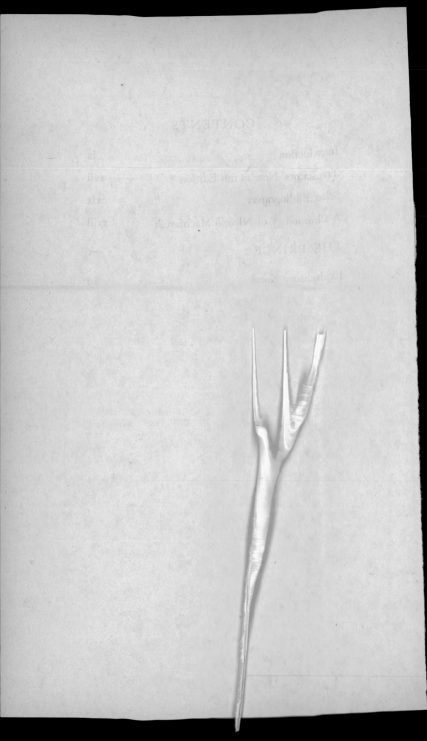

For Ignazio, Orlando, and Ambra

INTRODUCTION

THE PRINCE has generated polemical discussion ever since its appearance in the early sixteenth century. This slim volume has become a classic of modern social thought and a mainstay of courses on the great books, political theory, and Renaissance culture – and in all of these areas it continues to stimulate heated debate and controversy. While Machiavelli no doubt expected the critical tone of his treatise to provoke a sharp response among his readers, he might well have been surprised by the wide variety of different interpretations which have been suggested in the course of the last four centuries. The immediate practical purpose of *The Prince* was superseded within a decade of its composition, but its radically original treatment of crucial philosophical and political issues continues to attract new readers, many of whom are often unaware of any practical political goal Machiavelli might have intended in his argument.

While the work does contain a number of the key concepts of Machiavelli's mature political philosophy, it was never intended to represent a completely systematic exposition of all his views on the nature of politics. Machiavelli's theoretical speculations on the nature of the principality and its ruler in this book were limited, to some extent, by his more immediate goal – that of persuading the Medici family to conduct a crusade against the 'barbarian' invaders who had disrupted Italian life ever since the French invasion of 1494, an event which had turned Italy into the battleground of Europe, and to unify the many different principalities, duchies, and republics within the peninsula. Therefore, in a feverish state of enthusiasm and poetic inspiration, between July and December of 1513, Machiavelli interrupted his more lengthy commentary on Livy's history of republican Rome, which would eventually present his analysis of republican forms of government, to complete his more famous treatment of princely rule.

The year 1513 seemed to present the Medici with an excellent historical opportunity for fulfilling the role Machiavelli proposed for this family. In that same year, the son of Lorenzo de' Medici (Giovanni de' Medici), was elected to the papacy, taking the title of Leo X. The Pope's brother, Giuliano de' Medici, Duke of Nemours, seemed destined to consolidate the family's control of the Florentine government and its subject territories in Tuscany after the downfall of the republic for which Machiavelli had worked from 1498 until 1512. For a few brief but promising years, it seemed to Machiavelli and to many of his contemporaries that Medici power in Tuscany might be combined with Medici control of the Papal States and the Church's ample revenues. This fortuitous historical opportunity might well have provided the nucleus for the construction of an Italian state which could have successfully resisted foreign incursions and the eventual hegemony of non-Italian powers within the peninsula. To employ Machiavelli's own terms, the Medici were presented with a historical opportunity (*occasione*) that constituted a challenge to the ingenuity, ability, and skill (*virtù*) of their house. This challenge and this opportunity were the fleeting gifts of a benevolent fortune (*fortuna*), Machiavelli's metaphor for the contingencies in human history. In the course of offering such practical advice and specific political goals to the Medici, Machiavelli recast the traditional framework of medieval and humanist discourse on the nature of political leadership. As he himself put it, 'it seemed more suitable to me to search after the effectual truth of the matter rather than its imagined one... for there is such a gap between how one lives and how one ought to live that anyone who abandons what is done for what ought to be done learns his ruin rather than his preservation' (Chapter XV). It is no wonder that Machiavelli's contemporaries, accustomed to idealized portraits of benevolent Christian rulers, were shocked by his provocative vision of a prince unfettered by the constraints of traditional morality.

The author of *The Prince* had his own private reasons for dedicating such a work to his former Medici adversaries, since he hoped to become a participant in, if not the architect of, this grand political programme. He had served as secretary to the Florentine Republic under Piero Soderini, and after his dismissal from the government in 1512 following the return of the Medici to Florence, Machiavelli so longed to return to the

political arena that he wrote to a friend saying he would accept
any post offered him by the Medici, 'even if they start me off
by rolling stones'. With the deaths of Giuliano de' Medici in
1516, and of his successor Lorenzo de' Medici, Duke of Urbino,
in 1519, the possibilities for a successful realization of the
political goal proposed in the work were substantially dimin-
ished. As a result, Machiavelli never published the treatise
during his lifetime. It appeared posthumously in 1532, a year
after his *Discourses* were first published.

The publication of *The Prince* generated a complex debate
over its theoretical and moral implications that passed far
beyond a discussion of its immediate practical purpose and its
connection to the political fortunes and aspirations of the
Medici family. Moralists, particularly in England and France,
assailed the book as a compendium of cynical maxims fit only
for evil tyrants. Elizabethan writers were scandalized and
intrigued by what they saw as a typically Machiavellian
character – although the character was most often a Senecan
villain in doublet and hose. Their moral indignation was sometimes feigned, but the Elizabethans' nearly four hundred references to the Florentine secretary introduced the derogatory
terms 'Machiavellian' and 'Machiavellianism' into the English
language. Some churchmen branded the book the work of the
devil and its author an atheist, and Machiavelli's first name
came to be associated with an already popular term for the
devil: Old Nick. The book enjoyed the dubious distinction of
being attacked from all sides. It was placed on the Index by the
Catholic Church in 1559. Among Protestant reformers, it sym-
bolized all that was despised in the Italianate culture of High
Renaissance Europe: popery, the Roman Curia, 'reason of
state', the Society of Jesus (in anti-Catholic propaganda
Machiavelli was linked to Ignatius Loyola), and the moral
corruption that Europeans liked to localize within the Italian
peninsula but usually experienced closer to home.

As a result of this *succès de scandale*, *The Prince* became
known at least indirectly to every sixteenth- and seventeenth-
century reader. The traditional view of the 'Machiavellian'
Machiavelli finds its best expression in the dramatic literature
of the period: Machiavelli appears as a character in the prologue

of Marlowe's *The Jew of Malta* (1589), the embodiment of Machiavellian amorality, who remarks: 'I count religion but a childish toy, and hold there is no sin but ignorance.' More subtle Machiavellian figures include Shakespeare's Richard III and Iago.

In the seventeenth century, Machiavelli's original views on republican government began to be studied as assiduously as his interpretation of princely rule. James Harrington, Francis Bacon, and a host of minor thinkers began to acknowledge Machiavelli's contributions to republican theory and to political realism in *The Discourses*, *The Art of War*, and *The History of Florence*, and they questioned the traditional view of Machiavelli as a teacher of evil. During the Enlightenment, Frederick II of Prussia, at Voltaire's instigation, assailed Machiavelli's immorality, but other thinkers, including Hume, Rousseau, Montesquieu, and Alfieri, hailed the Florentine as the first modern thinker to have exposed the nature of political tyranny. Still later, during the Risorgimento, the period that led to the nineteenth-century unification of Italy, Italians saw the final chapter of *The Prince* as a harbinger of their new nation.

In our own century, the book has inspired a number of divergent and sometimes original interpretations. It has been variously read as the first work to analyse the role of the political élite; as the book which established the independence of politics from theology; as an early formulation of the political 'myth' required to galvanize apolitical masses into revolutionary action; as a practical guidebook containing timeless rules for the diplomat; and, of course, as the handbook of evil. These changing evaluations in our own era, as well as in the more distant past, probably reveal as much about the book's readers as they do about the author's intentions and ideas.

It is true that knowing the history of Machiavellianism and understanding the historical context of *The Prince* can help us avoid the wilful misreadings of the past. And yet no amount of historical scholarship has succeeded in explaining away the moral issues Machiavelli touches – particularly in his famous portrait of the new prince. For example, Machiavelli's choice of Cesare Borgia as the model for the new prince seemed scandalous later in the sixteenth century when the European reception of Francesco Guicciardini's *History of Italy* popularized the gossip about the incestuous relationships of Pope Alexander, Cesare, and Lucrezia Borgia, as well as their legendary murders. The simplistic formula used to summarize Machiavelli's complex view of politics and ethics ('the end justifies the means') is actually a gross mistranslation that has erected an almost insurmountable barrier to an understanding of Machiavelli's thought. The mere mention of this phrase conjures up a vision of power-mad rulers pursuing immoral ends by even more immoral means, but Machiavelli never spoke of justification here and merely remarked that 'in the actions of all men, and especially of princes, where there is no impartial arbiter, one must consider the final result' (*si guarda al fine*). Even in its correct form, the concept is of moral interest.

Machiavelli is subtler than some moralists have appreciated. He never imagined that *any* sort of political action could be justified, and he clearly pronounces his awareness of conventional moral exigencies. He condemns politicians whose only aim is power, who kill their fellow citizens, betray their friends, and who are without faith, mercy, or religion: 'By these means,' he says, 'one can acquire power but not glory.' Power does not confer glory, nor is might synonymous with right. The merely powerful are set apart from praiseworthy princes precisely because of the ends towards which they strive.

The only goal Machiavelli ever offers in all his works, *The Prince* included, that may excuse acts judged violent or immoral by traditional Christian standards is that of establishing a self-sufficient and stable body politic. The principality should be led by a prince who defends himself with an army of free citizens and who derives his power from the love of his subjects. Given a serious emergency (Italy's invasion by foreigners) and a unique historical opportunity to respond to this crisis by creating an Italian state through the Medici family, Machiavelli, the republican secretary, prefers external independence and internal stability to a weak republic endangered by foreign troops. As he remarks in *The Art of War*, ideal institutions are useless unless they are adequately protected, for they undergo 'the same sort of disorder as the rooms of a splendid and regal palace which, adorned with gems and gold but without a roof, have nothing to protect them from the rain'.

Extreme situations call for extreme measures, 'strong medicines', as he calls them. The new prince, if he is to be successful in defending a new Italian state, must learn *not* to be the good Christian prince; he must reject abstract, ideal, utopian schemes. States, Machiavelli believes, are not held with rosary beads in hand. Far from denying the existence of an ethical component in political life, Machiavelli suggests a new and revolutionary secular ethic that he takes to be a value incompatible with the equally stringent demands of traditional Christian morality: the establishment of an independent Italian state. In his readings of the classics, he had come to believe that Italy needed to revive the sense of shared community found in the ancient city-state; he sees republican Rome with her stalwart citizen-soldiers as the finest political institution to have evolved in the course of history. On the other hand, he recognizes the appeal of the system of moral values inherited from Christianity and from the tradition of natural law, even though he views this conventional morality as an impediment to the renaissance of the classical ideal of stable government.

Machiavelli permits little equivocation in our choice of which set of ethical principles and practical goals we should follow. There is little room for compromise between his new secular religion and that older faith directed towards the afterlife. If we are determined to make our way in the political realm, as he hopes any noble spirit would be, he warns us to do so armed with the attributes of 'the fox and the lion', and not as 'unarmed prophets' who fail for lack of the power to enforce belief in their ideals. With the sweep of his unforgettable metaphors, Machiavelli brushes aside much of political theory from Plato through St Thomas and the Christian humanists. Rather than providing an edifying picture of the Christian prince who rules his faithful subjects as a shepherd protects his docile flock, Machiavelli concentrates, instead, upon the world of power politics he observed as an emissary of the Florentine Republic to the courts of Europe.

Although he hopes that his prospective Medici patron will embrace his own noble patriotism, he is aware that such a realistic and pragmatic attitude in the hands of an unworthy man can be used for sinister purposes. Ironically, Machiavelli closes his treatise – after replacing a traditional set of moral values with a revolutionary set of political ideas and goals – with a religious tone and a biblical image. At the conclusion of *The Prince*, the man who would later declare in a private letter that he loved his country more than his soul assumes the role of the unarmed prophet without honour in his native land as he compares the establishment of an Italian state to the Exodus from Egypt and the opportunity fortune has bestowed upon the Medici to manna from heaven. Far from banishing religion from the realm of politics, Machiavelli has injected a religious fervour into the pursuit of secular political goals, with all its fateful implications for modern intellectual history.

Benedetto Croce once remarked that the dilemmas Machiavelli raised may never be resolved. Croce is right, and Machiavelli is partially responsible for igniting the controversy that followed the publication of his work. He made no attempt to systematize his opinions or to define carefully the traditional terms he uses in a revolutionary way. The very style of *The Prince* betrays the intuition of a genuine poet, not the rigour of a logical thinker. A memorable metaphor, a well-turned phrase, a rhetorical flourish, a colourful example may grab the reader's attention, but they appeal to emotion rather than intellect. Machiavelli's readers, in fact, have too often overlooked the logic of a position only imperfectly rendered in the author's impassioned rhetoric.

Machiavelli also failed to delineate the relationship between the new prince, who could establish a republic or a principality and thus reform corrupted institutions, and the republican form of government that Machiavelli himself always preferred. Because of the power of the polemical language in *The Prince*, the reasoned arguments in *The Discourses* – which contain his most original ideas on the constructive role of social conflict, on factions and conspiracies, and on corruption and reform – were largely ignored and have been adequately analysed only in the last few decades.

Yet Machiavelli's discussion of the often conflicting demands of public power and private morality was a real intellectual achievement. And his keen awareness of the role illusion and appearance play in affairs of state still provides an unusually precise picture of the realities of power, no matter in what era or by whom it is exercised. His personal political goal of a unified Italian state guided by the principles of political realism pointed toward the future. And it seems fair to conclude from what modern scholarship has unearthed of Machiavelli's life – his sincere patriotism, his chronic inability to follow his own sometimes cynical precepts in order to further his personal career, his candid and open manner employed with both friend and foe alike – that we may also absolve the author of *The Prince* from the charge that he was himself a 'Machiavellian'.

TRANSLATORS' NOTE

TO THIS EDITION

GIVEN the central place *The Prince* occupies in the history of political thought or its crucial role in Italian Renaissance culture, it is perhaps inevitable that most readers of the work in English translation concern themselves more with its ideas and content than with its form and style. However, Niccolò Machiavelli was a superb stylist, a political theorist whose best pages are always illuminated by the imagination of a poet and informed by a keen awareness of literary tradition. The present translation, substantially revised since its initial appearance in *The Portable Machiavelli* (Penguin, Harmondsworth, 1979), attempts to represent Machiavelli's ideas accurately and faithfully and to reflect the author's prose style as well. While many recent translators of *The Prince* have felt it necessary to shorten Machiavelli's ample periods in an attempt to simplify the text and to make it more attractive to contemporary readers, we have remained faithful, insofar as possible, to Machiavelli's more complex sentence structure. Great books have earned the right to make certain demands upon their readers, and Machiavelli's writing is never so obscure that it requires extensive modern editing of this kind.

Machiavelli's political vocabulary presents a vexing problem to any translator. Much of recent scholarship has quite rightly focused upon the several key terms employed in *The Prince* (one thinks immediately of publications by Fredi Chiappelli, Nicolai Rubinstein, J. H. Whitfield, Felix Gilbert, J. H. Hexter, Russell Price, Neal Wood, and a number of other scholars listed in the bibliography). Important terms such as *virtù, stato, occasione, fortuna, prudenza, libertà, ordini, vivere civile, gloria,* and *fantasia* often have no single and systematic equivalents in the English language. In fact, to explain the meaning of such individual terms in Machiavelli's work, entire critical articles are often required in order to cover all the possible meanings. *Virtù*, the best example, appears some sixty times in *The Prince* as a noun with a few additional occurrences as an adjective or adverb. It is evident from examining the context of these appearances that a faithful translator cannot consistently substitute one single English word for this flexible Italian term. In some cases, it is best rendered as 'ingenuity', 'skill', 'ability', or 'talent'; elsewhere, 'capacity', 'efficacy', 'qualities', 'strength', or 'power' seem best; and in a few instances, the English 'virtue' may, indeed, convey Machiavelli's meaning. A translator is always tempted to leave such terms in the original language, with lengthy explanatory notes. We feel, however, that translation is also a form of textual criticism, and that the translator must help to illuminate the text in another language. We have therefore chosen the path of rendering Machiavelli's difficult political vocabulary with English equivalents that best suit the context in which such difficult terms are found.

We should like to thank a number of colleagues and former students for their suggestions on the translation and, most especially, Mr Russell Price of the University of Lancaster for the helpful suggestions and corrections that were instrumental in preparing the final revision of this translation.

SELECT BIBLIOGRAPHY

ITALIAN EDITIONS: Italian editions of Machiavelli's works are numerous. The most useful edition of the major writings is to be found in the one-volume *Tutte le opere* (Sansoni, Florence, 1972), edited by Mario Martelli. For a complete edition in eleven volumes, consult the collected works magnificently edited by Sergio Bertelli, *Niccolò Machiavelli: Opera omnia* (Edizioni Valdonega, Verona, 1968–80), the tenth volume of which comprises a bibliography and the last volume a detailed index.

ENGLISH TRANSLATIONS: For the most recent collection of new translations from Machiavelli's various political, historical, and literary works, see Peter Bondanella and Mark Musa, eds. and trans., *The Portable Machiavelli* (Penguin, Harmondsworth, 1979); *The Prince and Other Political Writings*, ed. Bruce Penman (Dent, London, 1981), is a similar anthology which omits any literary works. For additional translations not contained in either of these anthologies, consult Allan H. Gilbert, ed. and trans., *Machiavelli: The Chief Works and Others*, 3 vols. (Duke University Press, Durham. N.C., 1965). A number of excellent editions of *The Prince* are available in separate editions: James B. Atkinson, ed. and trans., *The Prince* (Bobbs-Merrill, Indianapolis, Ind., 1976); George Bull, ed. and trans., *The Prince* (Penguin, Harmondsworth, 1961, rev. ed. 1975); and Thomas G. Bergin, ed. and trans., *The Prince* (AHM Publishing Corporation, Northbrook, Ill., 1947).

MACHIAVELLI'S BIOGRAPHY AND INTELLECTUAL BACKGROUND: The classic study of Machiavelli's life is Roberto Ridolfi's *The Life of Niccolò Machiavelli* (Routledge & Kegan Paul, London, 1963), although Pasquale Villari's *The Life and Times of Niccolò Machiavelli*, 2 vols. (Greenwood Press, London, rpt. of 1892 ed.) is still worth examining. Three briefer surveys of Machiavelli's life and works are J. R. Hale's *Machiavelli and Renaissance Italy* (Penguin, Harmondsworth, 1972); Quentin Skinner's *Machiavelli* (Oxford University Press, Oxford, 1981); and Silvia Russo-Fiore's *Niccolò Machiavelli* (Twayne, Boston, 1982). For specific studies of Machiavelli's career in the Florentine Chancery and the political milieu within which he worked there, see the following: Nicolai Rubinstein,

'The Beginnings of Niccolò Machiavelli's Career in the Florentine Chancery', *Italian Studies* 11 (1956), 72–91; Fredi Chiappelli, 'Machiavelli as Secretary', *Italian Quarterly* 14 (1970), 27–44; and Sergio Bertelli, 'Constitutional Reforms in Renaissance Florence', *Journal of Medieval and Renaissance Studies* 3 (1973), 139–64, as well as 'Machiavelli and Soderini', *Renaissance Quarterly* 28 (1975), 1–16. For the political and intellectual context of Machiavelli's work, there are numerous books and articles, but the following are especially useful: Allan Gilbert, *Machiavelli's Prince and Its Forerunners: The Prince as a Typical Book 'De Regimine Principum'* (Duke University Press, Durham, N.C., 1938); Federico Chabod, *Machiavelli and the Renaissance* (Bowes and Bowes, London, 1958); Felix Gilbert, *Machiavelli and Guicciardini: Politics and History in Sixteenth-Century Florence* (Princeton University Press, Princeton, 1965), and a series of important essays in *History: Choice and Commitment* (Harvard University Press, London, 1977); Rudolf von Albertini, *Firenze dalla repubblica al principato* (Einaudi, Turin, 1970); Myron Gilmore, ed., *Studies on Machiavelli* (Sansoni, Florence, 1972); J. H. Hexter, *The Vision of Politics on the Eve of the Reformation: More, Machiavelli, Seyssel* (Allen Lane, London, 1973); J. A. G. Pocock, *The Machiavellian Moment: Florentine Political Thought and the Atlantic Republican Tradition* (Princeton University Press, Princeton, 1975); and Quentin Skinner, *The Foundations of Modern Political Thought*, 2 vols. (Cambridge University Press, Cambridge, 1978). John Najemy, 'Machiavelli and the Medici: The Lessons of Florentine History', *Renaissance Quarterly* 35 (1982), 551–76, is useful for Machiavelli's relationship to this important family.

MACHIAVELLI'S IDEALS, POLITICAL TERMINOLOGY, AND STYLE: A number of general works are available in both English and Italian. Franco Fido's *Machiavelli* (Palumbo, Palermo, 1965) contains an interesting collection of critical materials on Machiavelli from his times to the present; other collections of recent studies include: Martin Fleisher, ed., *Machiavelli and the Nature of Political Thought* (Atheneum, New York, 1972); and Anthony Parel, ed., *The Political Calculus: Essays on Machiavelli's Philosophy* (University of Toronto Press, Toronto, 1972). Leo Strauss' *Thoughts on Machiavelli* (University of Washington Press, London, 1969) as well as two books by J. H. Whitfield – *Machiavelli* (Blackwells, Oxford, 1947), and *Discourses on Machiavelli* (W. Heffer, Cambridge, 1969) – can be relied upon to challenge and exasperate the reader. In addition,

Sydney Anglo, *Machiavelli: A Dissection* (Gollancz, London, 1969) and Alfredo Bonadeo, *Corruption, Conflict, and Power in the Works and Times of Niccolò Machiavelli* (University of California Press, Berkeley, 1973) are useful. Three Italian works of importance covering the entire range of Machiavelli's thought are: Gennaro Sasso, *Niccolò Machiavelli: Storia del suo pensiero politico* (Mulino, Bologna, 1980); Ugo Dotti, *Niccolò Machiavelli: La fenomenologia del potere* (Feltrinelli, Milan, 1979); and Carlo Dionisotti, *Machiavellerie: Storia e fortuna di Machiavelli* (Einaudi, Turin, 1980). For recent French scholarship on Machiavelli, see Claude Lefort, *Le travail de l'œuvre Machiavel* (Gallimard, Paris, 1972) and Bernard Guillemain, *Machiavel: L'anthropologie politique* (Droz, Geneva, 1977). Much of recent criticism on Machiavelli has focused upon his political terminology. In addition to the previously cited works by Hexter and Whitfield, an early innovator in this area is Fredi Chiappelli, *Studi sul linguaggio del Machiavelli* (Il Saggiatore, Florence, 1952). For other analyses of *virtù*, consult: Neal Wood, 'Machiavelli's Concept of *Virtù* Reconsidered,' *Political Studies* 15 (1967), 159–72; I. Hannaford, 'Machiavelli's Concept of *Virtù* in *The Prince* and *The Discourses* Reconsidered,' *Political Studies* 20 (1972), 185–9; and Russell Price, 'The Senses of *Virtù* in Machiavelli,' *European Studies Review* 3 (1973), 315–45. *Fortuna* is perceptively analysed in Timothy J. Lukes, 'Fortune Comes of Age (in Machiavelli's Literary Works),' *The Sixteenth-Century Journal* 11 (1980), 33–50. *Gloria* is studied by Russell Price, 'The Theme of *Gloria* in Machiavelli,' *Renaissance Quarterly* 30 (1977), 588–631, and by Victor Santi, *La 'gloria' nel pensiero di Machiavelli* (Longo, Ravenna, 1979); Machiavelli's notion of 'liberty' receives attention from Marcia L. Colish, 'The Idea of Liberty in Machiavelli,' *The Journal of the History of Ideas* 32 (1971), 323–50. *Ambizione* is treated by Russell Price in '*Ambizione* in Machiavelli's Thought', *History of Political Thought* 3 (1982), 383–445. J. Samuel Preus outlines Machiavelli's views on religion in 'Machiavelli's Functional Analysis of Religion: Context and Object,' *The Journal of the History of Ideas* 40 (1979), 171–90. For studies of how Machiavelli's style is shaped by his historical views and his diplomatic career, see Peter Bondanella, *Machiavelli and the Art of Renaissance History* (Wayne State University Press, Detroit, 1974); Jean-Jacques Marchand, *Niccolò Machiavelli: i primi scritti politici (1499–1512)* (Editrice Antenore, Padua, 1975); and Gian Mario Anselmi, *Ricerche sul Machiavelli storico* (Pacini Editore, Pisa, 1979).

MACHIAVELLI'S INFLUENCE: Again, the literature is extensive. For several available works in English which provide an excellent point of departure, see: Friedrich Meinecke, *Machiavellism: The Doctrine of Raison D'Etat and Its Place in Modern History* (Routledge & Kegan Paul, London, 1957); Mario Praz, *The Flaming Heart* (Doubleday, Garden City, N.Y., 1958); and Felix Raab, *The English Face of Machiavelli: A Changing Interpretation 1500–1700* (Routledge & Kegan Paul, London, 1964). In Italian, see Josef Macek, *Machiavelli e il Machiavellismo* (La Nuova Italia, Florence, 1980).

A CHRONOLOGY OF
NICCOLÒ MACHIAVELLI

1469	Niccolò di Bernardo Machiavelli is born in Florence
1498	Machiavelli is appointed and subsequently elected to head the Second Chancery of the Republic of Florence; shortly thereafter, he receives an additional post as secretary to the Ten of War and Peace
1500	Machiavelli completes his first diplomatic mission to France, meeting King Louis XII and Georges d'Amboise, Cardinal of Rouen
1502–3	Machiavelli completes diplomatic missions to Cesare Borgia in the Romagna and Rome, witnessing Borgia's fall from power after the death of his father, Pope Alexander VI
1504	Machiavelli returns to France
1506	Machiavelli is sent on a diplomatic mission by the republic to Pope Julius II
1507–8	Machiavelli undertakes his first mission to Emperor Maximilian
1512	Soderini's republic is overthrown and the Medici return to power in Florence
1513	Dismissed from office and narrowly escaping serious punishment, Machiavelli retires to his country place in Sant' Andrea in Percussina; he begins *The Discourses* and completes *The Prince*
1513–17	Machiavelli completes *The Discourses*
1515–16 (?)	*The Art of War* is completed
1518 (?)	Machiavelli composes *The Mandrake Root*, his greatest literary work
1519 (?)	The first printed edition of *The Mandrake Root* appears
1520	After writing *The Life of Castruccio Castracani*, Machiavelli is awarded the commission to write a history of Florence by the university of Florence
1521	*The Art of War* is published, the only one of Machiavelli's political works to appear in print during his lifetime

1525	Another comedy, *Clizia*, is staged; Machiavelli also probably composed his *Discourse or Dialogue on Language* at this time, although the work's authorship is disputed
1526	*The History of Florence* is presented to Pope Clement VII
1527	Machiavelli dies and is buried in Santa Croce in Florence
1531	*The Discourses* is posthumously published
1532	*The Prince* is posthumously published
1559	Machiavelli's works are placed on the Index of Prohibited Books
1640	*The Prince* receives its first published English translation by Edward Dacres

THE PRINCE

CONTENTS

CONTENTS

DEDICATORY PREFACE

*Niccolò Machiavelli to
Lorenzo de' Medici, the Magnificent**

IN most instances, it is customary for those who desire to win
the favour of a Prince to present themselves to him with those
things they value most or which they feel will most please him;
thus, we often see princes given horses, arms, vestments of gold
cloth, precious stones, and similar ornaments suited to their
greatness. Wishing, therefore, to offer myself to Your Magnificence with some evidence of my devotion to you, I have not
found among my belongings anything that I might value more
or prize so much as the knowledge of the deeds of great men,
which I have learned from a long experience in modern affairs
and a continuous study of antiquity; having with great care
and for a long time thought about and examined these deeds,
and now having set them down in a little book, I am sending
them to Your Magnificence.

And although I consider this work unworthy of your station,
I am sure, nevertheless, that your humanity will move you to
accept it, for there could not be a greater gift from me than to
give you the means to be able, in a very brief time, to understand all that I, in many years and with many hardships and
dangers, have come to understand and to appreciate. I have
neither decorated nor filled this work with fancy sentences,
with rich and magnificent words, or with any other form of
rhetorical or unnecessary ornamentation which many writers
normally use in describing and enriching their subject matter;
for I wished that nothing should set my work apart or make it
pleasing except the variety of its material and the seriousness of
its contents. Neither do I wish that it be thought presumptuous
if a man of low and inferior station dares to debate and to
regulate the rule of princes; for, just as those who paint land-
scapes place themselves in a low position on the plain in order

to consider the nature of the mountains and the high places and place themselves high atop mountains in order to study the plains, in like manner, to know well the nature of the people one must be a prince, and to know well the nature of princes one must be of the people.

Accept, therefore, Your Magnificence, this little gift in the spirit that I send it; if you read and consider it carefully, you will discover in it my most heartfelt desire that you may attain that greatness which fortune and all your own capacities promise you. And if Your Magnificence will turn your eyes at some time from the summit of your high position toward these lowlands, you will realize to what degree I unjustly suffer a great and continuous malevolence of fortune.

CHAPTER I

How Many Kinds of Principalities There Are and the Way They Are Acquired

ALL states, all dominions that have had and continue to have power over men were and still are either republics or principalities. Principalities are either hereditary, in which instance the family of the prince has ruled for generations, or they are new. The new ones are either completely new, as was Milan for Francesco Sforza,* or they are like members added to the hereditary state of the prince who acquires them, as is the Kingdom of Naples for the King of Spain.* Dominions taken in this way are either used to living under a prince or are accustomed to being free; and they are gained either by the arms of others or by one's own, either through fortune or through ingenuity.

CHAPTER II

On Hereditary Principalities

I SHALL set aside any discussion of republics, because I treated them elsewhere at length.* I shall consider solely the principality, developing as I go the topics mentioned above; and I shall discuss how these principalities can be governed and maintained.

I say, then, that in hereditary states accustomed to the rule of their prince's family there are far fewer difficulties in maintaining them than in new states; for it suffices simply not to break ancient customs, and then to suit one's actions to unexpected events; in this manner, if such a prince is of ordinary ability, he will always maintain his state, unless some extraordinary and inordinate force deprive him of it; and although it may be taken away from him, he will regain it with the slightest mistake of the usurper.

As an example, we have in Italy the Duke of Ferrara,* who withstood the assaults of the Venetians in 1484 and those of Pope Julius* in 1510 for no other reason than the tradition of his rule in that dominion. Because a prince by birth has fewer reasons and less need to harm his subjects, it is natural that he should be more loved; and if no unusual vices make him hated, it is reasonable and natural that he be well liked by them. And in the antiquity and continuity of his rule, the records and causes of innovations die out, because one change always leaves space for the construction of another.*

CHAPTER III

On Mixed Principalities

But it is the new principality that causes difficulties. In the first place, if it is not completely new but is instead an acquisition (so that the two parts together may be called mixed), its difficulties derive from one natural problem inherent in all new principalities: men gladly change their masters, thinking to better themselves; and this belief causes them to take arms against their ruler; but they fool themselves in this, since with experience they see that things have become worse. This stems from another natural and ordinary necessity, which is that a new prince must always offend his new subjects both through his soldiers and other countless injuries that are involved in his new conquest; thus, you have made enemies of all those you injured in occupying the principality and you are unable to maintain as friends those who helped you to rise to power, since you cannot satisfy them in the way that they had supposed, nor can you use strong measures* against them, for you are in their debt; because, although one may have the most powerful of armies, he always needs the support of the inhabitants to seize a province. For these reasons, Louis XII, King of France,* quickly occupied Milan and just as quickly lost it; and the first time, the troops of Ludovico* alone were needed to retake it from him, because those citizens who had opened the gates of the city to the king, finding themselves deceived in their beliefs and in that future improvement they had anticipated, could not support the offences of the new prince.

It is indeed true that when lands which have rebelled once are taken a second time, it is more difficult to lose them; for the lord, taking advantage of the revolt, is less reticent about punishing offenders, ferreting out suspects, and shoring up weak positions. So that, if only a Duke Ludovico threatening the borders was sufficient for France to lose Milan the first time, the whole world* had to oppose her and destroy her armies or chase them from Italy to cause her to lose it the second time; and this happened for the reasons mentioned above. Nevertheless, it was taken from her both the first and the second time.

The general explanations for the first loss have been discussed; now there remains to specify those for the second, and to see what remedies the King of France had, and those that one in the same situation might have, so that he might be able to maintain a stronger grip on his conquest than did France. Therefore, I say that those dominions which, upon being conquered, are added to the long-established state of him who acquires them are either of the same province and language or they are not. When they are, it is easier to hold them, especially when they are unaccustomed to freedom; and to possess them securely, it is only necessary to have extinguished the family line of the prince who ruled them, because in so far as other things are concerned, men live peacefully as long as their old way of life is maintained and there is no change in customs: thus, we have seen what happened in the case of Burgundy, Brittany, Gascony, and Normandy,* which have been part of France for such a long time; and although there are some linguistic differences, nevertheless the customs are similar and they have been able to get along together easily. And anyone who acquires these lands and wishes to maintain them must bear two things in mind: first, that the family line of the old prince must be extinguished; second, that neither their laws nor their taxes be altered; as a result they will become in a very brief time one body with the old principality.

But when dominions are acquired in a province that is not similar in language, customs, and laws, it is here that difficulties arise; and it is here that one needs much good fortune and much diligence to hold on to them. And one of the best and most efficacious remedies would be for the person who has taken possession of them to go and live there. This would make that possession more secure and durable, as the Turks did with Greece; for despite all the other precautions they took to retain that dominion, if they had not gone there to live, it would have been impossible for them to hold on to it. Because, by being on the spot, one sees trouble at its birth and one can quickly remedy it; not being there, one hears about it after it has grown and there is no longer any remedy. Moreover, the province would not be plundered by one's own officers; the subjects would be pleased to have direct recourse to their prince; thus, wishing to be good subjects, they have more reason to love him and, wanting to be otherwise, more reason to fear him. Anyone who might wish to invade that dominion from abroad would be more hesitant; so that, living right there, the prince can only with the greatest of difficulties lose it.

The other and better solution is to send colonies into one or two places that will act as supports for your own state; for it is necessary that the prince either do this or maintain a large number of infantry and cavalry. Colonies do not cost much, and with little or no expense a prince can send and maintain them; and in so doing he hurts only those whose fields and houses have been taken and given to the new inhabitants, who are only a small part of that state; and those that he hurts, being dispersed and poor, can never be a threat to him, and all others remain on the one hand unharmed (and because of this, they should remain silent), and on the other afraid of making a mistake, for fear that what happened to those who were dispossessed might happen to them. I conclude that these colonies are not expensive, they are more faithful, and they create fewer difficulties; and those who are hurt cannot pose a threat, since they are poor and scattered, as I have already said. Concerning this, it should be noted that one must either pamper or do away with men, because they will avenge themselves for minor offences while for more serious ones they cannot; so that any harm done to a man must be the kind that removes any fear of revenge. But by maintaining soldiers there instead of colonies, one spends much more, being obliged to consume all the revenues of the state in guarding its borders, so that the profit becomes a loss; and far greater injury is committed, since the entire state is harmed by the army changing quarters from one place to another; everybody resents this inconvenience, and everyone becomes an enemy; and these are enemies that can be harmful, since they remain, although conquered, in their own home. And so, in every respect, this kind of defence is as useless as the other kind, colonization, is useful.

Moreover, anyone who is in a province that is unlike his own in the ways mentioned above should make himself the leader and defender of the less powerful neighbours and do all he can to weaken those who are more powerful, and he should be careful that, for whatever reason, no foreigner equal to himself in strength enter there. And it will always happen that the outsider will be brought in by those who are dissatisfied, either because of too much ambition or because of fear, as was once seen when the Aetolians brought the Romans into Greece,* and in every other province that the Romans entered, they were brought in by the inhabitants. What occurs is that as soon as a powerful foreigner enters a province, all who are less powerful cling to him, moved by the envy they have for the one who has ruled over them; so that, concerning these weaker powers, he has no trouble whatsoever in winning them over, since all of them will immediately and willingly become part of the state that he has acquired. He has only to be on his guard that they do not seize too much power and authority; and, with his force and their support, he can very easily put down those who are powerful, and remain complete arbiter of that province. And anyone who does not follow this procedure will quickly lose what he has taken, and while he holds it, he will find it full of infinite difficulties and worries.

In the provinces that they seized, the Romans followed these methods very carefully; they sent colonies, had dealings with the less powerful without increasing their strength, put down the powerful, and did not allow powerful foreigners to gain prestige there. And I shall cite only the province of Greece as an example: the Romans kept the Achaeans and the Aetolians in check; the Macedonian kingdom was put down;* Antiochus was driven out;* nor were they ever persuaded by the merits of the Achaeans or the Aetolians to allow them any gain of territory; nor did the persuasion of Philip of Macedonia ever convince them to make him their friend without first humbling him; nor could the power of Antiochus force their consent to his having any authority whatsoever in that province. For the Romans did in these instances what all wise princes should do: these princes have not only to watch out for present problems but also for those in the future, and try diligently to avoid them; for once problems are recognized ahead of time, they can be easily cured; but if you wait for them to present themselves, the medicine will be too late, for the disease will have become incurable. And what physicians say about disease* is applicable here: that at the beginning a disease is easy to cure but difficult to diagnose; but as time passes, not having been recognized or treated at the outset, it becomes easy to diagnose but difficult to cure. The same thing occurs in affairs of state; for by recognizing from afar the diseases that are spreading in the state (which is a gift given only to the prudent ruler), they can be cured quickly; but when they are not recognized and are left to grow to the extent that everyone recognizes them, there is no longer any cure.

Thus, seeing trouble from afar, the Romans always found a remedy; and they never allowed such trouble to develop unopposed, in order to avoid a war, because they knew that war cannot be avoided but can only be put off to the advantage of others; therefore, they wanted to go to war with Philip and Antiochus in Greece in order not to have to combat them in Italy; and they could have, at the time, avoided both the one and the other, but they did not want to. Nor did they ever like what is always on the tongues of our wise men today, to enjoy the benefits of time, but they enjoyed instead the benefits of their strength and prudence; for time brings with it all things, and it can bring with it the good as well as the bad and the bad as well as the good.

But let us return to France and determine if she did any of the things we have just mentioned; and I shall speak of Louis and not of Charles;* and therefore about the one whose progress has been observed better because he held territory in Italy for a longer period, and you will see that he did the contrary of those things that must be done in order to hold one's rule in a foreign province.

King Louis was installed in Italy because of the ambition of the Venetians, who wanted by his coming to gain for themselves half of Lombardy. I will not criticize the enterprise the King undertook; for, wishing to establish a first foothold in Italy and not having any friends in this land and, furthermore, having all the gates closed to him because of the actions of King Charles, he was forced to strike up whatever friendships he could; and this worthy undertaking would have succeeded if he had not erred in his other moves. After having taken Lombardy, then, the King immediately regained the prestige that Charles had lost him: Genoa surrendered; the Florentines became his allies; the Marquis of Mantua, the Duke of Ferrara, the Bentivogli, the Countess of Forlì, the lords of Faenza, Pesaro, Rimini, Camerino, and Piombino, and the people of Lucca, Pisa, and Siena all rushed to gain his friendship.* And at that point the Venetians could see the recklessness of the enterprise they had undertaken; in order to acquire a bit of Lombardy, they had made the King the master of a third of Italy.

Consider, now, with what little trouble the King might have maintained his reputation in Italy if he had followed the rules listed above and kept secure and defended all those friends of his who, there being a goodly number of them, both weak and fearful, some of the Church, others of the Venetians, were always forced to be his allies; and through them he could have easily secured himself against the remaining great powers. But no sooner was he in Milan than he did the contrary, giving assistance to Pope Alexander so that he could seize Romagna. Nor did he realize that with this decision he had made himself weaker, abandoning his allies and those who had thrown themselves into his lap, and made the Church stronger by adding to it so much temporal power in addition to the spiritual power from which it derives so much authority. And having made an initial mistake, he was obliged to make others; so that in order to put an end to the ambition of Alexander and to keep him from becoming lord of Tuscany, he was forced to come to Italy. He was not satisfied to have made the Church powerful and to have lost his allies, for, coveting the Kingdom of Naples, he divided it with the King of Spain; and where he first had been the arbiter of Italy, he brought in a partner so that the ambitious and the malcontents of that province had someone else to turn to; and where he could have left a figurehead king to rule that kingdom, he replaced him, establishing one there who could, in turn, drive Louis out.

The desire to acquire is truly a very natural and normal thing; and when men who are able do so, they will always be praised and not condemned; but when they cannot and wish to do so at any cost, herein lies the error and the blame. If France, therefore, could have assaulted Naples with her own troops, she should have done so; if she could not, she should not have shared it. And if the division of Lombardy with the Venetians deserves to be overlooked, since it allowed Louis to gain a foothold in Italy, the other division deserves to be criticized, since it cannot be excused by necessity.

Thus, Louis had made these five mistakes: he had destroyed the weaker powers; he increased the power of another force in Italy; he had brought into that province a powerful foreigner; he did not come there to live; and he did not send colonies there. In spite of this, these mistakes, had he lived, might not have damaged him if he had not made a sixth: that of reducing the Venetians' power; for if he had not made the Church stronger, nor brought Spain into Italy, it would have been most reasonable and necessary to put them down; but, having taken those first initiatives, he should never have agreed to their ruin; for as long as they were powerful they would have always kept the others from trying to seize Lombardy, partly because the Venetians would not have allowed this unless they themselves became the rulers of Lombardy, and partly because the others would not have wanted to take it away from France to give it to the Venetians; and they would not have had the nerve to provoke both of them. And if someone were to say: King Louis relinquished Romagna to Alexander and the Kingdom of Naples to Spain in order to avoid a war, I would reply with the arguments given above: that one should never allow chaos to develop in order to avoid going to war, because one does not avoid a war but instead puts it off to his disadvantage. And if some others were to note the promise that the King had made the Pope to undertake that enterprise in return for the annulment of his marriage and for the Cardinal's hat of Rouen,* I should answer with what I shall say further on about the promises of princes and how they should be observed.

King Louis lost Lombardy, therefore, by not following any of the principles observed by others who had taken provinces and who wished to retain them. Nor is this in any sense a miracle, but very ordinary and understandable. And I spoke about this at Nantes* with the Cardinal of Rouen when Valentino (for this was what Cesare Borgia, son of Pope Alexander,* was commonly called) occupied Romagna; for when the Cardinal of Rouen told me that Italians understood little about war, I replied to him that the French understood little about politics; for if they did understand, they would not permit the Church to gain so much power. And we have learned through experience that the power of the Church and of Spain in Italy has been caused by France, and that her downfall has been brought about by them. From this one can derive a general rule which rarely, if ever, fails: that anyone who is the cause of another's becoming powerful comes to ruin himself, because that power is the result either of cunning or of force, and both these two qualities are suspect to the one who has become powerful.

CHAPTER IV

Why the Kingdom of Darius, Occupied by Alexander, Did Not Rebel Against His Successors after the Death of Alexander

CONSIDERING the difficulties one has in maintaining a newly acquired state, one might wonder how it happened that when Alexander the Great,* having become lord of Asia in a few years and having hardly occupied it, died – wherefore it would have seemed reasonable for the whole state to revolt – Alexander's successors nevertheless managed to hold on to it; and they had, in keeping it, no other difficulty than that which originated among themselves from their own ambition. Let me reply that all principalities known to us are governed in one of two different ways: either by a prince with the others as his servants, who, as ministers, through his favour and permission, assist in governing that kingdom; or by a prince and barons who hold that position not because of any favour of their master but because of the nobility of their birth. Such barons as these have their own dominions and subjects who recognize them as masters and are naturally fond of them. Those dominions governed by a prince and his ministers hold their prince in greater authority, for in all his province there is no one that may be recognized as superior to him; and if they do obey any other, they do so as his minister and officer, and they do not harbour any special affection for him.

Examples of these two different kinds of governments in our own times are the Turkish Emperor and the King of France. The entire kingdom of the Turk is ruled by one master; the others are his servants; and dividing his kingdom into parts, he sends various administrators there, and he moves them and changes them as he pleases. But the King of France is placed among a group of established nobles who are recognized in that state by their subjects and who are loved by them; they have their hereditary rights; the King cannot remove them without danger to himself. Anyone, therefore, who considers these two states will find that the difficulty lies in taking possession of the Turkish state, but once it has been conquered, it is very simple to retain it. On the other hand, you will find that in some ways it is easier to seize the French state, but it is extremely difficult to hold on to it.

The reasons for the difficulty in being able to occupy the Turkish kingdom are that it is not possible to be summoned there by the rulers of that kingdom, nor to hope to make your enterprise easier with the rebellion of those the ruler has around him. This is because of the reasons mentioned above: since they are all slaves and dependent on the ruler, it is more difficult to corrupt them; and even if they were corrupted, you cannot hope that they will be very useful, not being able to attract followers for the reasons already discussed. Therefore, anyone who attacks the Turks must consider that he will find them completely united, and he must rely more on his own strength than on their lack of unity. But once beaten and broken in battle so that they cannot regroup their troops, there is nothing else to be feared but the family of the prince; once it is extinguished, there remains no one else to be feared, for the others have no credit with the people; and just as the victor before the victory could not place hope in them, so he need not fear them afterwards.

The opposite occurs in kingdoms governed like France, because you can enter them with ease once you have won to your side some baron of the kingdom; for you always find malcontents and those who desire a change; these people, for the reasons already given, can open the way to that state and facilitate your victory. However, wishing to hold on to it is accompanied by endless problems, problems with those that have aided you and with those you have suppressed; nor does it suffice to do away with the family of the prince, because the lords who make themselves heads of new factions still remain; and you lose that state at the first occasion, for you are neither able to make them happy nor are you able to do away with them.

Now, if you will consider the type of government Darius established, you will find it similar to the kingdom of the Turks; and therefore Alexander first had to overwhelm it

totally and defeat it in battle; after this victory, Darius being
dead, that state remained securely in Alexander's hands for the
reasons discussed above. And his successors, had they been
united, could have enjoyed it with ease; for in that kingdom no
disorders arose other than those they themselves had caused.
But in states organized like France, it is impossible to hold
them with such ease. Because of this, there arose the frequent
revolts of Spain, France, and Greece against the Romans, all
because of the numerous principalities that were in those states;
as long as the memory of them lasted, the Romans were always
unsure of their power; but once that memory had been extinguished, because of their long and powerful rule, they became
sure possessors. Afterwards, when the Romans fought among
themselves, each one was able to draw a following from those
provinces, according to the authority he enjoyed there; and
since the families of their former rulers had been extinguished,
they recognized only the Romans. Taking all these things into
account, therefore, no one at all should marvel at the ease with
which Alexander retained the state of Asia, or at the problems
that others suffered in preserving their acquisition, such as
Pyrrhus* and many others. This is not caused by the greater
or lesser skill of the victor but rather by the difference of the
situations.

CHAPTER V

How Cities or Principalities Should be Governed that Lived by Their Own Laws Before They Were Occupied

As I have said, when those states that are acquired are used to
living by their own laws and in freedom, there are three
methods of holding on to them: the first is to destroy them; the
second is to go there in person to live; the third is to allow
them to live with their own laws, forcing them to pay a tribute
and creating therein a government made up of a few people
who will keep the state friendly toward you. For such a govern-

ment, having been created by that prince, knows it cannot last without his friendship and his power, and it must do everything possible to maintain them; and a city used to living in freedom is more easily maintained through the means of its own citizens than in any other way, if you decide to preserve it.

As examples, there are the Spartans and the Romans. The Spartans held Athens and Thebes by building therein a government consisting of a few people; eventually they lost them both. The Romans, in order to hold Capua, Carthage, and Numantia, destroyed them and did not lose them; they wished to hold Greece in almost the same manner as the Spartans held it, making it free and leaving it under its own laws, and they did not succeed; thus, they were obliged to destroy many of the cities in that province in order to retain it. For, in fact, there is no secure means of holding on to them except by destroying them. And anyone who becomes lord of a city used to living in liberty and does not destroy it may expect to be destroyed by it, because such a city always has as a refuge, in any rebellion, the spirit of liberty and its ancient institutions, neither of which is ever forgotten either because of the passing of time or because of the bestowal of benefits. And it matters little what one does or foresees, since if one does not separate or scatter the inhabitants, they will not forget that spirit or those institutions; and immediately, in every case, they will return to them just as Pisa did* after one hundred years of being held in servitude by the Florentines. But when cities or provinces are accustomed to living under a prince and the family of that prince has been extinguished, they, being on the one hand used to obedience and, on the other, not having their old prince and not being able to agree on choosing another from amongst themselves, yet not knowing how to live as free men, are as a result hesitant in taking up arms, and a prince can win them over and assure himself of their support with greater ease. But in republics there is greater vitality, greater hatred, greater desire for revenge; the memory of ancient liberty does not and cannot allow them to submit, so that the most secure course is either to destroy them or to go there to live.

CHAPTER VI

On New Principalities Acquired by One's Own Arms and Skill

No one should marvel if, in speaking of principalities that are totally new as to their prince and organization, I use the most illustrious examples; since men almost always tread the paths made by others and proceed in their affairs by imitation, although they are not completely able to stay on the path of others nor attain the skill of those they imitate, a prudent man should always enter those paths taken by great men and imitate those who have been most excellent, so that if one's own skill does not match theirs, at least it will have the smell of it; and he should proceed like those prudent archers* who, aware of the strength of their bow when the target they are aiming at seems too distant, set their sights much higher than the designated target, not in order to reach to such a height with their arrow but rather to be able, with the aid of such a high aim, to strike the target.

I say, therefore, that in completely new principalities, where there is a new prince, one finds in maintaining them more or less difficulty according to the greater or lesser skill of the one who acquires them. And because this act of transition from private citizen to prince presupposes either ingenuity or fortune,* it appears that either the one or the other of these two things should, in part, mitigate many of the problems; nevertheless, he who relies upon fortune less maintains his position best. Things are also facilitated when the prince, having no other dominions to govern, is constrained to come to live there in person. But to come to those who, by means of their own skill and not because of fortune, have become princes, I say that the most admirable are Moses, Cyrus, Romulus, Theseus, and the like.* And although we should not discuss Moses, since he was a mere executor of things ordered by God, nevertheless he must be admired, if for nothing but that grace which made him worthy of talking with God. But let us consider Cyrus and the others who have acquired or founded kingdoms; you will find them all admirable; and if their deeds and their particular institutions are considered, they will not appear different from those of Moses, who had so great a guide. And examining their deeds and their lives, one can see that they received nothing from fortune except the opportunity, which gave them the material they could mould into whatever form they desired; and without that opportunity the strength of their spirit would have been extinguished, and without that strength the opportunity would have come in vain.

It was therefore necessary for Moses to find the people of Israel in Egypt slaves and oppressed by the Egyptians in order that they might be disposed to follow him to escape this servitude. It was necessary for Romulus not to stay in Alba and to be exposed at birth so that he might become King of Rome and founder of that nation. It was necessary for Cyrus to find the Persians discontented with the empire of the Medes, and the Medes soft and effeminate after a lengthy peace. Theseus could not have shown his skill if he had not found the Athenians scattered. These opportunities, therefore, made these men successful, and their outstanding ingenuity made that opportunity known to them, whereby their nations were ennobled and became prosperous.

Like these men, those who become princes through their skill acquire the principality with difficulty, but they hold on to it easily; and the difficulties they encounter in acquiring the principality grow, in part, out of the new institutions and methods they are obliged to introduce in order to found their state and their security. And one should bear in mind that there is nothing more difficult to execute, nor more dubious of success, nor more dangerous to administer than to introduce a new order of things; for he who introduces it has all those who profit from the old order as his enemies, and he has only lukewarm allies in all those who might profit from the new. This lukewarmness partly stems from fear of their adversaries, who have the law on their side, and partly from the scepticism of men, who do not truly believe in new things unless they have actually had personal experience of them. Therefore, it happens that whenever those who are enemies have the chance to attack, they do so enthusiastically, whereas those others defend hesitantly, so that they, together with the prince, are in danger.

It is necessary, however, if we desire to examine this subject thoroughly, to observe whether these innovators act on their own or are dependent on others: that is, if they are forced to beg or are able to use power in conducting their affairs. In the first case, they always come to a bad end and never accomplish anything; but when they depend on their own resources and can use power, then only seldom do they find themselves in peril. From this comes the fact that all armed prophets were victorious and the unarmed came to ruin. Besides what has been said, people are fickle by nature; and it is simple to convince them of something but difficult to hold them in that conviction; and, therefore, affairs should be managed in such a way that when they no longer believe, they can be made to believe by force. Moses, Cyrus, Theseus, and Romulus could not have made their institutions long respected if they had been unarmed; as in our times happened to Brother Girolamo Savonarola,* who was ruined by his new institutions when the populace began no longer to believe in them, since he had no way of holding steady those who had believed nor of making the disbelievers believe. Therefore, such men have great problems in getting ahead, and they meet all their dangers as they proceed, and they must overcome them with their skill; but once they have overcome them and have begun to be respected, having removed those who were envious of their merits, they remain powerful, secure, honoured, and happy.

To such noble examples I should like to add a minor one; but it will have some relation to the others, and I should like it to suffice for all similar cases: and this is Hiero of Syracuse.* From a private citizen, this man became the prince of Syracuse; he did not receive anything from fortune except the opportunity, for since the citizens of Syracuse were oppressed, they elected him as their leader; and from that rank he proved himself worthy of becoming their prince. And he was so skilful while still a private citizen that someone who wrote about him said 'that he lacked nothing to reign save a kingdom.' He did away with the old militia and established a new one; he put aside old friendships and made new ones; and since he had allies and soldiers that depended on him, he was able to construct whatever building he wished on such a foundation; so that it cost him great effort to acquire and little to maintain.

CHAPTER VII

On New Principalities Acquired with the Arms of Others and by Fortune

THOSE private citizens who become princes through fortune alone do so with little effort, but they maintain their position only with a great deal; they meet no obstacles along their way since they fly to success, but all their problems arise when they have arrived. And these are the men who are granted a state either because they have money or because they enjoy the favour of him who grants it: this occurred to many in Greece in the cities of Ionia and the Hellespont, where Darius created princes in order that he might hold these cities for his security and glory; in like manner were set up those emperors who from private citizens came to power by bribing the soldiers. Such men depend solely upon two very uncertain and unstable things: the will and the fortune of him who granted them the state; they do not know how and are not able to maintain their position. They do not know how, since if men are not of great intelligence and ingenuity, it is not reasonable that they know how to rule, having always lived as private citizens; they are not able to, since they do not have forces that are friendly and faithful. Besides, states that rise quickly, just as all the other things of nature that are born and grow rapidly, cannot have roots and ramifications; the first bad weather kills them, unless these men who have suddenly become princes, as I have noted, are of such ability that they know how to prepare themselves quickly and to preserve what fortune has put in their laps, and to construct afterwards those foundations that others have built before becoming princes.

Regarding the two methods just listed for becoming a

prince, by skill or by fortune, I should like to offer two recent examples: these are Francesco Sforza and Cesare Borgia. Francesco, through the required means and with a great deal of ingenuity, became Duke of Milan from his station as a private citizen, and that which he had acquired with countless hardships he maintained with little trouble. On the other hand, Cesare Borgia (commonly called Duke Valentino) acquired the state through the favour and help of his father, and when this no longer existed, he lost it,* and this despite the fact that he did everything and used every means that a prudent and skilful man ought to use in order to root himself securely in those states that the arms and fortune of others had granted him. Because, as stated above, anyone who does not lay his foundations beforehand could do so later only with great skill, although this would be done with inconvenience to the architect and danger to the building. If, therefore, we consider all the steps taken by the Duke, we shall see that he laid sturdy foundations for his future power; and I do not judge it useless to discuss them, for I would not know of any better precepts to give to a new prince than the example of his deeds; and if he did not succeed in his plans, it was not his fault but was instead the result of an extraordinary and extreme instance of ill fortune.

Alexander VI, in his attempts to advance his son, the Duke, had many problems, both present and future. First, he saw no means of making him master of any state that did not already belong to the Church; and if he attempted to seize anything belonging to the Church, he knew that the Venetians and the Duke of Milan would not agree to it because Faenza and Rimini were already under the protection of the Venetians. Moreover, he saw that the troops of Italy, and especially those he would have to use, were in the hands of those who had reason to fear the Pope's power; and he could not count on them, since they were all Orsini, Colonnesi, and their allies.* Therefore, he had to disturb the order of things and cause turmoil among these states in order securely to make himself master of a part of them. This was easy for him to do, for he found that the Venetians, moved by other motives, had decided to bring the French back into Italy; not only did he not oppose this, but he rendered it easier by annulling King Louis' first marriage. The King, therefore, entered Italy with the aid of the Venetians and the consent of Alexander; and no sooner was he in Milan than the Pope procured troops from him for the Romagna campaign; these were granted to him because of the reputation of the King.

Having seized, then, Romagna and having beaten the Colonna, the Duke, wishing to maintain his gain and to advance further, was held back by two things: first, his troops' lack of loyalty; second, the will of France; that is, the troops of the Orsini, which he had been using, might let him down and not only keep him from acquiring more territory but even take away what he had already conquered; and the King, as well, might do the same. He had one experience like this with the Orsini soldiers, when, after the seizure of Faenza, he attacked Bologna and saw them go reluctantly into battle; as for the King, he learned his purpose when he invaded Tuscany after the capture of the Duchy of Urbino; the King forced him to abandon that campaign. As a consequence, the Duke decided to depend no longer upon the arms and favour of others. And his first step was to weaken the Orsini and Colonna factions in Rome; he won over all their followers who were noblemen, making them his own noblemen and giving them huge subsidies; and he honoured them, according to their rank, with military commands and civil appointments; as a result, in a few months their affection for the factions died out in their hearts and all of it was turned towards the Duke. After this, he waited for the opportunity to do away with the Orsini leaders, having already scattered those of the Colonna family; and good opportunity arose and the use he put it to was even better: for when the Orsini later realized that the greatness of the Duke and of the Church meant their ruin, they called together a meeting at Magione, in Perugian territory. From this resulted the rebellion of Urbino and the uprisings in Romagna, and endless dangers for the Duke, all of which he overcame with the aid of the French. And when his reputation had been regained, placing no trust either in France or other outside forces, in order not to have to test them, he turned to deceptive methods. And he knew how to falsify his intentions so well that the Orsini themselves, through Lord Paulo, made peace with him; the Duke did not fail to use all kinds of gracious acts to reassure Paulo, giving him money, clothing, and horses, so that the stupidity of the Orsini brought them to Sinigaglia and into his hands.* Having killed these leaders and having changed their allies into his friends, the Duke had laid very good foundations for his power, having all of Romagna along with the Duchy of Urbino, and, more important, it appeared that he had befriended Romagna and had won the support of all of its populace once the people began to taste the beneficial results of his rule.

And because this matter is notable and worthy of imitation by others, I shall not pass it over. After the Duke had taken Romagna and had found it governed by powerless lords who had been more anxious to plunder their subjects than to govern them and had given them reason for disunity rather than unity, so that the entire province was full of thefts, fights, and of every other kind of insolence, he decided that if he wanted to make it peaceful and obedient to the ruler's law it would be necessary to give it good government. Therefore, he put Messer Remirro de Orco,* a cruel and able man, in command there and gave him complete authority. This man, in little time, made the province peaceful and united, and in doing this he made for himself a great reputation. Afterwards, the Duke decided that such great authority was no longer required, for he was afraid that it might become odious; and he set up in the middle of the province a civil court with a very distinguished president, wherein each city had its own counsellor. And because he realized that the rigorous measures of the past had generated a certain amount of hatred, he wanted to show, in order to purge men's minds and to win them to his side completely, that if any form of cruelty had arisen, it did not originate from him but from the harsh nature of his minister. And having found the occasion to do this, one morning at Cesena he had Messer Remirro placed on the piazza in two pieces with a block of wood and a bloody sword beside him. The ferocity of such a spectacle left those people satisfied and amazed at the same time.

But let us return to where we digressed. I say that the Duke, finding himself very powerful and partially secured from present dangers, having armed himself the way he wanted to, and having in large measure destroyed those nearby forces that might have harmed him, still had to take into account the King of France if he wished to continue his conquests, for he realized that the King, who had become aware of his error too late, would not support further conquest. And because of this, he began to seek out new allies and to temporize with France during the campaign the French undertook in the Kingdom of Naples against the Spaniards who were besieging Gaeta. His intent was to make himself secure against them; and he would have quickly succeeded in this if Alexander had lived.

And these were his methods concerning present things. But as for future events, he had first to fear that a new successor in control of the Church might not be his friend and might try to take away from him what Alexander had given him. Against this possibility he thought to secure himself in four ways: first, by putting to death all the relatives of those lords that he had dispossessed in order to prevent the Pope from employing that opportunity; second, by gaining the friendship of all the noblemen of Rome, as already mentioned, in order to hold the Pope in check by means of them; third, by making the College of Cardinals as much his own as he could; fourth, by acquiring such a large territory before the Pope died that he would be able to resist an initial attack without need of allies. Of these four things, he had achieved three by the time of Alexander's death; the fourth he had almost achieved, for he killed as many of the dispossessed noblemen as he could seize, and very few saved themselves; and he had won over the Roman noblemen; and he had a great following in the College of Cardinals; and as for the acquisition of new territory, he had planned to become lord of Tuscany and was already in possession of Perugia and Piombino and had taken Pisa under his protection. And as soon as he no longer needed to respect the wishes of France (for he no longer had to, since the French had already been deprived of the kingdom by the Spaniards, so that it was necessary for both of them to purchase his friendship), he would attack Pisa. After this, Lucca and Siena would have immediately surrendered, partly to spite the Florentines and partly out of fear, and the Florentines would have had no means of preventing it.

If he had carried out these designs (and he would have brought them to fruition during the same year that Alexander died), he would have gathered together so many forces and such a reputation that he would have been able to stand alone and would no longer have had to rely upon the favour and forces of others, but rather on his own power and ingenuity. But Alexander died five years after he had drawn his sword. He left his son, gravely ill, with only the state of Romagna secured and with all the others up in the air, between two very powerful enemy armies. And there was in the Duke so much ferocity and so much ability, and so well did he understand how men can be won or lost, and so firm were the foundations that he had laid in such a short time, that if he had not had those armies upon him or if he had been healthy, he would have overcome every difficulty. And that his foundations were good is witnessed by the fact that Romagna waited more than a month for him; in Rome, although only half alive, he was safe; and although the Baglioni, the Vitelli, and the Orsini came to Rome, they found none of their allies opposed to him; if he could not set up a Pope he wanted, at least he could act to ensure that it would not be a man he did not want. But if he had been healthy at the time of Alexander's demise, everything would have been simple. And he himself said to me, on the day when Julius II was made Pope, that he had thought of what might happen on his father's death, and he had found a remedy for everything, except he never dreamed that at the time of his father's death he too would be at death's door.

Now, having summarized all of the Duke's actions, I would not know how to censure him; on the contrary, I believe I am correct in proposing that he be imitated by all those who have risen to power through fortune and with the arms of others. Because he, possessing great courage and high aims, could not have conducted himself in any other manner; and his plans were frustrated solely by the brevity of Alexander's life* and by his own illness. Anyone, therefore, who determines it necessary in his newly acquired principality to protect himself from his enemies, to win friends, to conquer either by force or by fraud, to make himself loved and feared by the people, to be followed and respected by his soldiers, to put to death those who can or may do him harm, to replace ancient institutions with new ones, to be severe and gracious, magnanimous and generous, to do away with unfaithful soldiers and to select new ones, to maintain the friendship of kings and of princes in such a way that they must assist you gladly or offend you with caution – that person cannot find more recent examples than this man's deeds. One can only censure him for making Julius Pope; in this he made a bad choice, since, as I said before, not being able to elect a Pope of his own, he could have kept anyone he wished from the papacy; and he should have never agreed to raising to the papacy any cardinal he might have offended or who, upon becoming Pope, might have cause to fear him. For men do harm either out of fear or hatred. Those he had injured were, among others, San Pietro ad Vincula, Colonna, San Giorgio, Ascanio;* any of the others, upon becoming Pope, would have to fear him, except for Rouen and the Spaniards; the latter because they were related to him and were in his debt, the former because of his power, since he was joined to the kingdom of France. Therefore, the Duke, above all else, should have made a Spaniard Pope; failing in that, he should have agreed to the election of Rouen* and not to that of San Pietro ad Vincula. And anyone who believes that new benefits make men of high station forget old injuries is deceiving himself. The Duke, then, erred in this election, and it was the cause of his ultimate downfall.

CHAPTER VIII

On Those Who Have Become Princes Through Wickedness

BUT because there are yet two more ways one can from an ordinary citizen become prince, which cannot completely be attributed to either fortune or skill, I believe they should not be left unmentioned, although one of them will be discussed at greater length in a treatise on republics. These two are: when one becomes prince through some wicked and nefarious means or when a private citizen becomes prince of his native city through the favour of his fellow citizens. And in discussing the first way, I shall cite two examples, one from classical times and the other from recent days, without otherwise entering into the merits of this method, since I consider them sufficient for anyone forced to imitate them.

Agathocles the Sicilian,* not only from being an ordinary citizen but from being of low and abject status, became King of Syracuse. This man, a potter's son, lived a wicked life at every stage of his career; yet he joined to his wickedness such strength of mind and of body that, when he entered upon a military career, he rose through the ranks to become commander of Syracuse. Once placed in such a position, having decided to become prince and to hold with violence and without any obligations to others what had been granted to him by universal consent, and having made an agreement with Hamilcar the Carthaginian, who was waging war with his armies in Sicily, he called together one morning the people and the senate of Syracuse as if he were going to discuss things concerning the state; and with a prearranged signal, he had his troops kill all the senators and the richest citizens; and when they were dead, he seized and held the rule of the city without any opposition from the citizenry. And although he was twice defeated by the Carthaginians and eventually besieged, not only was he able to defend his city but, leaving part of his troops for the defence of the siege, with his other men he attacked Africa, and in a short time he freed Syracuse from the siege and forced the Carthaginians into dire straits: they were obliged to make peace with him and to be content with possession of Africa and to leave Sicily to Agathocles.

Anyone, therefore, who examines the deeds and the life of this man will observe nothing or very little that can be attributed to fortune; since, as was said earlier, not with the aid of others but by rising through the ranks, which involved a thousand hardships and dangers, did he come to rule the principality which he then maintained by many brave and dangerous actions. Still, it cannot be called ingenuity* to kill one's fellow citizens, to betray friends, to be without faith, without mercy, without religion; by these means one can acquire power but not glory. For if one were to consider Agathocles's ability in getting into and out of dangers, and his greatness of spirit in supporting and in overcoming adversaries, one can see no reason why he should be judged inferior to any most excellent commander; nevertheless, his vicious cruelty and inhumanity, along with numerous wicked deeds, do not permit us to honour him among the most excellent of men. One cannot, therefore, attribute to either fortune or skill what he accomplished without either the one or the other.

In our own days, during the reign of Alexander VI, Oliverotto of Fermo, who many years before had been left as a child without a father, was brought up by his maternal uncle, Giovanni Fogliani. While still very young he was sent to serve as a soldier under Paulo Vitelli so that, once he was versed in that skill, he might attain some outstanding military position. Then, after Paulo died, he served under his brother, Vitellozzo; and in a very brief time, because of his intelligence and his vigorous body and mind, he became the commander of his troops. But since he felt it was servile to work for others, he decided to seize Fermo with the aid of some citizens of Fermo who preferred servitude to the liberty of their native city, and with the assistance of the followers of Vitellozzo; and he wrote to Giovanni Fogliani that, having been away many years from home, he wished to come to see him and his city and to inspect his own inheritance; and since he had exerted himself for no other reason than to acquire glory, he wanted to arrive in honourable fashion, accompanied by an escort of a hundred horsemen from among his friends and servants so that his fellow citizens might see that he had not spent his time in vain; and he begged his uncle to arrange for an honourable reception from the people of Fermo, one which might bring honour not only to Giovanni but also to himself, being his pupil. Giovanni, therefore, in no way failed in his duty toward his nephew: he had him received in honourable fashion by the people of Fermo, and he gave him rooms in his own house. Oliverotto, after a few days had passed and he had secretly made the preparations necessary for his forthcoming wickedness, gave a magnificent banquet to which he invited Giovanni Fogliani and all of the first citizens of Fermo. And when the meal and all the other entertainment customary at such banquets were completed, Oliverotto, according to plan, began to discuss serious matters, speaking of the greatness of Pope Alexander and his son, Cesare, and of their undertakings. After Giovanni and the others had replied to his comments, he suddenly rose up, announcing that these were matters to be discussed in a more secluded place; and he retired into another room, followed by Giovanni and all the other citizens. No sooner were they seated than from secret places in the room out came soldiers who killed Giovanni and all the others. After this murder, Oliverotto mounted his horse, paraded through the town, and besieged the chief officials in the government palace; so that out of fear they were forced to obey him and to constitute a government of which he made himself prince. And when all those were killed who, because they were discontented, might have harmed him, he strengthened himself by instituting new civil and military institutions; so that, in the space of the year that he held the principality, not only was he secure in the city of Fermo, but he had become feared by all its neighbours. His expulsion would have been as difficult as that of Agathocles if he had not permitted himself to be tricked by Cesare Borgia, when at Sinigaglia, as was noted above, the Duke captured the Orsini and the Vitelli; there he, too, was captured, a year after he committed the parricide, and together with Vitellozzo, who had been his teacher in ingenuity and wickedness, he was strangled.

One might wonder how Agathocles and others like him, after so many betrayals and cruelties, could live for such a long time secure in their cities and defend themselves from outside enemies without being plotted against by their own citizens; many others, using cruel means, were unable even in peaceful times to hold on to their state, not to speak of the uncertain times of war. I believe that this depends on whether cruelty be well or badly used. Well used are those cruelties (if it is permitted to speak well of evil) that are carried out in a single stroke, done out of necessity to protect oneself, and are not continued but are instead converted into the greatest possible benefits for the subjects. Badly used are those cruelties which, although being few at the outset, grow with the passing of time instead of disappearing. Those who follow the first method can remedy their condition with God and with men as Agathocles did; the others cannot possibly survive.

Wherefore it is to be noted that in taking a state its conqueror should weigh all the harmful things he must do and do them all at once so as not to have to repeat them every day, and in not repeating them to be able to make men feel secure and win them over with the benefits he bestows upon them. Anyone who does otherwise, either out of timidity or because of poor advice, is always obliged to keep his knife in his hand; nor can he ever count upon his subjects, who, because of their fresh and continual injuries, cannot feel secure with him. Injuries, therefore, should be inflicted all at the same time, for the less they are tasted, the less they offend; and benefits should be distributed a bit at a time in order that they may be savoured fully. And a prince should, above all, live with his subjects in such a way that no unforeseen event, either good or bad, may make him alter his course; for when emergencies arise in adverse conditions, you are not in time to resort to cruelty, and that good you do will help you little, since it will be judged a forced measure and you will earn from it no thanks whatsoever.

CHAPTER IX

On the Civil Principality

BUT coming to the second instance, when a private citizen, not through wickedness or any other intolerable violence, but with the favour of his fellow citizens, becomes prince of his native city (this can be called a civil principality, the acquisition of which neither depends completely upon skill nor upon fortune, but instead upon a mixture of shrewdness and luck), I maintain that one reaches this princedom either with the favour of the common people or with that of the nobility. For these two different humours are found in every body politic; and they arise from the fact that the people do not wish to be commanded or oppressed by the nobles, and the nobles desire to command and to oppress the people; and from these two opposed appetites there arises one of three effects: either a principality or liberty or anarchy.

A principality is brought about either by the common people or by the nobility, depending on which of the two parties has the opportunity. For when the nobles see that they cannot resist the populace, they begin to support one among them and make him prince in order to be able, under his protection, to satisfy their appetites. The common people as well, seeing that they cannot resist the nobility, give their support to one man and make him prince in order to have the protection of his authority. He who attains the principality with the aid of the nobility maintains it with more difficulty than he who becomes prince with the assistance of the common people, for he finds himself a prince amidst many who feel themselves to be his equals, and because of this he can neither govern nor manage them as he wishes. But he who attains the principality through popular favour finds himself alone and has around him either no one or very few who are not ready to obey him. Moreover, one cannot honestly satisfy the nobles without harming others, but the common people can certainly be satisfied: their desire is more just than that of the nobles – the former want not to be oppressed and the latter want to oppress. Moreover, a prince can never make himself secure when the people are his enemy because they are so many; he can make himself secure against the nobles because they are so few. The worst that a prince can expect from a hostile people is to be abandoned by them; but with a hostile nobility not only does he have to fear being abandoned but also that they will unite against him; for, being more perceptive and shrewder, they always have time to save themselves, to seek the favours of the side they believe will win. Furthermore, a prince must always live with the same common people; but he can easily do without the same nobles, having the power to create them and to destroy them from day to day and to take away and give back their prestige as he sees fit.

And in order to clarify this point better, I say that the nobles should be considered chiefly in two ways: either they conduct themselves in such a way that they commit themselves completely to your cause or they do not. Those who commit themselves and are not greedy should be honoured and loved; those who do not commit themselves can be analysed in two ways. They act in this manner out of fear and a natural lack of courage, in which case you should make use of them, especially those who are wise advisers, since in prosperous times they will gain you honour and in adverse times you need not fear them. But when, cunningly and influenced by ambition, they refrain from committing themselves to you, this is a sign that they think more of themselves than of you; and the prince should be wary of such men and fear them as if they were open enemies, because they will always, in adverse times, help to bring about his downfall.

However, one who becomes prince with the support of the common people must keep them as his friends; this is easy for him, since the only thing they ask of him is not to be oppressed. But one who, against the will of the common people, becomes prince with the assistance of the nobility should, before all else, seek to win the people's support, which should be easy if he takes them under his protection. And because men, when they are well treated by those from whom they expected harm, are more obliged to their benefactor, the common people quickly become better disposed toward him than if he had become prince with their support. And a prince can gain their favour in various ways, but because they vary according to the situation no fixed rules can be given for them, and therefore I shall not talk about them. I shall conclude by saying only that a prince must have the friendship of the common people; otherwise he will have no support in times of adversity.

Nabis,* prince of the Spartans, withstood the attacks of all of Greece and of one of Rome's most victorious armies, and he defended his city and his own rule against them, and when danger was near he needed only to protect himself from a few of his subjects; but if he had had the common people against him, this would not have been sufficient. And let no one dispute my opinion by citing that trite proverb, 'He who builds upon the people builds upon the mud', because that is true when a private citizen lays his foundations and allows himself to believe that the common people will free him if he is oppressed by enemies or by the public officials (in this case a man might often find himself deceived, like the Gracchi of Rome* or like

Messer Giorgio Scali* of Florence); but when the prince who builds his foundations on the people is one who is able to command and is a man of spirit, not bewildered by adversities, and does not lack other necessities, and through his courage and his institutions keeps up the spirits of the populace, he will never find himself deceived by the common people, and he will discover that he has laid sound foundations.

Principalities of this type are usually endangered when they are about to change from a proper civil society to an absolute form of government. For these princes either rule by themselves or by means of public officials; in the latter case their position is weaker and more dangerous since they depend entirely upon the will of those citizens who are appointed to hold the offices; these men, especially in adverse times, can very easily seize the state either by open opposition or by disobedience. And in such times of danger the prince has no time for taking absolute control, for the citizens and subjects who are used to receiving their orders from public officials are, in these crises, not willing to obey his orders; and in doubtful times he will always find a scarcity of men he can trust. Such a prince cannot rely upon what he sees during periods of calm, when the citizens need his rule, because then everyone comes running, makes promises, and each one is willing to die for him – since death is unlikely; but in times of adversity, when the state needs its citizens, then few are to be found. And this experiment is all the more dangerous in that it can be made but once. And, therefore, a wise prince should think of a method by which his citizens, at all times and in every circumstance, will need the assistance of the state and of himself; and then they will always be loyal to him.

CHAPTER X

How the Strength of All Principalities Should Be Measured

IN analysing the qualities of these principalities, another consideration must be discussed; that is, whether the prince has so much power that he can, if necessary, stand on his own, or whether he always needs the protection of others. And in order to clarify this section, I say that I judge those princes self-sufficient who, either through abundance of troops or of money, are able to gather together a suitable army and fight a good battle against whoever should attack them; and I consider those who always need the protection of others to be those who cannot meet their enemy in the field, but must seek refuge behind their city walls and defend them. The first case has already been treated, and later on I shall say whatever else is necessary on the subject.* Nothing more can be added to the second case than to encourage such princes to fortify and provision their cities and not to concern themselves with the surrounding countryside. And anyone who has well fortified his city and has well managed his affairs with his subjects in the manner I detailed above (and discuss below*) will be besieged only with great caution; for men are always enemies of undertakings in which they foresee difficulties, and it cannot seem easy to attack someone whose city is well fortified and who is not hated by his people.

The cities of Germany are completely free, they have little surrounding territory, they obey the emperor when they wish, and they fear neither him nor any other nearby power, as they are fortified in such a manner that everyone thinks their capture would be a tedious and difficult affair. For they all have sufficient moats and walls; they have adequate artillery; they always store in their public warehouses enough to drink and to eat and to burn for a year; and besides all this, in order to be able to keep the lower classes fed without exhausting public funds, they always have in reserve a year's supply of raw materials sufficient to give these people work at those trades which are the nerves and the lifeblood of that city and of the industries from which the people earn their living. Moreover, they hold the military arts in high regard, and they have many regulations for maintaining them.

Therefore, a prince who has a strong city and who does not make himself hated cannot be attacked; and even if he were to be attacked, the enemy would have to depart in shame, for human affairs are so changeable that it is almost impossible that one maintain a siege for a year with his troops idle. And if it is objected that if the people have their possessions outside the city and see them destroyed, they will lose patience, and the long siege and self-interest will cause them to forget their prince, I reply that a powerful and spirited prince will always overcome all such difficulties, inspiring his subjects now with the hope that the evil will not last long, now with the fear of the enemy's cruelty, now by protecting himself with clever manoeuvres against those who seem too outspoken. Besides this, the enemy will naturally burn and waste the surrounding country on arrival, just when the spirits of the defenders are still ardent and determined on the city's defence; and thus the prince needs to fear so much the less, because after a few days, when their spirits have cooled down a bit, the damage has already been inflicted and the evils suffered, and there is no means of correcting the matter; and now the people will rally around their prince even more, for it would appear that he is bound to them by obligations, since their homes were burned and their possessions wasted in his defence. And the nature of men is such that they find themselves obligated as much for the benefits they confer as for those they receive. Thus, if everything is taken into consideration, it will not be difficult for a prudent prince to keep high the spirits of his citizens from the beginning to the conclusion of the siege, so long as he does not lack enough food and the means for his defence.

CHAPTER XI

On Ecclesiastical Principalities

THERE remain now only the ecclesiastical principalities to be discussed: concerning these, all the problems occur before they are acquired; for they are acquired either through ability or through fortune and are maintained without either; they are sustained by the ancient institutions of religion, which are so powerful and of such a kind that they keep their princes in power in whatever manner they act and live their lives. These princes alone have states and do not defend them, subjects and do not rule them; and the states, remaining undefended, are never taken away from them; and the subjects, being ungoverned, show no concern, and they do not think about, nor are they able to sever, their ties with them. These principalities, then, are the only secure and happy ones. But since they are protected by higher causes that the human mind is unable to reach, I shall not discuss them; for, being exalted and maintained by God, it would be the act of a presumptuous and foolhardy man to discuss them. Nevertheless, someone might ask me why it is that the Church, in temporal matters, has arrived at such power when, until the time of Alexander, the Italian powers – not just those who were the established rulers, but every baron and lord, no matter how weak – considered her temporal power as insignificant, and now a King of France trembles before it and it has been able to throw him out of Italy and to ruin the Venetians; although this situation may already be known, it does not seem superfluous to me to recall it in some detail.

Before Charles, King of France, came into Italy, this country was under the rule of the Pope, the Venetians, the King of Naples, the Duke of Milan, and the Florentines. These rulers had to keep two major problems in mind: first, that a foreigner could enter Italy with his armies; second, that no one of them increase his territory. Those whom they needed to watch most closely were the Pope and the Venetians. And to restrain the

Venetians the alliance of all the rest was necessary, as was the case in the defence of Ferrara; and to keep the Pope in check they made use of the Roman barons, who, divided into two factions, the Orsini and the Colonna, always had a reason for squabbling amongst themselves; they kept the papacy weak and unstable, standing with their weapons in hand right under the Pope's eyes. And although from time to time there arose a courageous Pope like Pope Sixtus,* neither fortune nor his wisdom could ever free him from these inconveniences. And the brevity of the reigns of the popes was the cause; for in ten years, the average life expectancy of a Pope, he might with difficulty put down one of the factions; and if, for example, one Pope had almost extinguished the Colonna, a new Pope who was the enemy of the Orsini would emerge, enabling the Colonna to grow powerful again, and yet he would not have time enough to destroy the Orsini.

As a consequence, the temporal powers of the Pope were little respected in Italy. Then Alexander VI came to power, and he, more than any of the popes who ever reigned, showed how well a Pope, with money and troops, could succeed; and he achieved, with Duke Valentino as his instrument and the French invasion as his opportunity, all those things that I discussed earlier in describing the actions of the Duke. And although his intention was not to make the Church great but rather the Duke, nevertheless what he did resulted in the increase of the power of the Church, which, after his death and once the Duke was destroyed, became the heir of his labours. Then came Pope Julius,* and he found the Church strong, possessing all of Romagna, having destroyed the Roman barons, and, by Alexander's blows, having snuffed out their factions; and he also found the way open for the accumulation of wealth by a method never before used by Alexander or his predecessors. These practices Julius not only continued but intensified; and he was determined to take Bologna, to crush the Venetians, and to drive the French from Italy, and he succeeded in all these undertakings; and he is worthy of even more praise, since he did everything for the increased power of the Church and not for any particular individual. He also managed to keep the Orsini and the Colonna factions in the same condition in which he found them; and although there were some leaders among them who wanted to make changes, there were two things which held them back: one, the power of the Church, which frightened them; and, two, not having any of their own family as cardinals, for these were the source of the conflicts among them. These factions will never be at peace as long as they have cardinals, since such men foster factions, both in Rome and outside it, and those barons are compelled to defend them; and thus, from the ambitions of the prelates are born the discords and the tumults among the barons. Therefore, His Holiness Pope Leo* has found the papacy very powerful in-deed; and it is to be hoped that if his predecessors made it great by feats of arms, he will, through his bounty and his infinite virtues, make it very great and worthy of reverence.

CHAPTER XII

On the Various Kinds of Troops and Mercenary Soldiers

HAVING treated in detail all the characteristics of those princi-palities which I proposed to discuss at the beginning, and having considered, to some extent, the reasons for their success or shortcomings, and having demonstrated the ways by which many have tried to acquire them and to maintain them, it remains for me now to speak in general terms of the kinds of offence and defence that can be adopted by each of the previ-ously mentioned principalities. We have said above that a prince must have laid firm foundations; otherwise he will of necessity come to grief. And the principal foundations of all states, the new as well as the old or mixed, are good laws and good armies. And since there cannot exist good laws where there are no good armies, and where there are good armies there must be good laws, I shall leave aside the treatment of laws and discuss the armed forces.

Let me say, therefore, that the armies with which a prince de-fends his state are made up of his own people, or of mercenaries, or auxiliaries, or of mixed troops. Mercenaries and auxiliaries are useless and dangerous. And if a prince holds on to his state by means of mercenary armies, he will never be stable or secure; for they are disunited, ambitious, without discipline, disloyal; they are brave among friends; among enemies they are cowards; they have no fear of God, they keep no faith with men; and your downfall is deferred only so long as the attack is deferred; and in peace you are plundered by them, in war by your enemies. The reason for this is that they have no other love nor other motive to keep them in the field than a meagre wage, which is not enough to make them want to die for you. They love being your soldiers when you are not making war, but when war comes they either flee or desert. This would require little effort to demonstrate, since the present ruin of Italy is caused by nothing other than her dependence for a long period of time on mercenary forces. These forces did, at times, help some get ahead, and they appeared courageous in combat with other mercenaries; but when the invasion of the foreigner came they showed themselves for what they were; and thus, Charles, King of France, was permitted to take Italy with a piece of chalk.* And the man who said that our sins were the cause of this disaster spoke the truth;* but they were not at all those that he had in mind, but rather these that I have described; and because they were the sins of princes, the princes in turn have suffered the penalty for them.

I wish to demonstrate more fully the sorry nature of such armies. Mercenary captains are either excellent soldiers or they are not; if they are, you cannot trust them, since they will always aspire to their own greatness either by oppressing you, who are their masters, or by oppressing others against your intent; but if the captain is without skill, he usually ruins you. And if someone were to reply that anyone who bears arms will act in this manner, mercenary or not, I would answer that armies have to be commanded either by a prince or by a republic: the prince must go in person and perform the duties of a captain himself; the republic must send its own citizens; and when they send one who does not turn out to be an able man, they must replace him; if he is capable, they ought to restrain him with laws so that he does not go beyond his authority. And we see from experience that only princes and armed republics make very great advances, and that mercenaries do nothing but harm; and a republic armed with its own citizens is less likely to come under the rule of one of its citizens than a city armed with foreign soldiers.

Rome and Sparta for many centuries stood armed and free. The Swiss are extremely well armed and are completely free. An example from antiquity of the use of mercenary troops is the Cathaginians; they were almost overcome by their own mercenary soldiers after the first war with the Romans, even though the Carthaginians had their own citizens as officers. Philip of Macedonia* was made captain of their army by the Thebans after the death of Epaminondas,* and after the victory he took their liberty from them. The Milanese, after the death of Duke Philip, employed Francesco Sforza to war against the Venetians; having defeated the enemy at Caravaggio, he joined with them to oppress the Milanese, his employers. Sforza, his father, being in the employ of Queen Giovanna of Naples,* all at once left her without defences; hence, in order not to lose her kingdom, she was forced to throw herself into the lap of the King of Aragon. And if the Venetians and the Florentines have in the past increased their possessions with such soldiers, and their captains have not yet made themselves princes but have instead defended them, I answer that the Florentines have been favoured in this matter by luck; for among their able captains whom they could have had reason to fear, some did not win, others met with opposition, and others turned their ambition elsewhere. The one who did not win was John Hawkwood,* whose loyalty, since he did not succeed, will never be known; but anyone will admit that had he succeeded, the Florentines would have been at his mercy. Sforza always had the Bracceschi* as enemies so that each checked the other. Francesco turned his ambition to Lombardy, Braccio against the Church and the Kingdom of Naples.

But let us come to what has occurred just recently. The Florentines made Paulo Vitelli* their captain, a very able man and one who rose from private life to achieve great fame. If this man had taken Pisa, no one would deny that the Florentines would have had to become his ally; for, if he had become employed by their enemies, they would have had no defence, and if they had kept him on, they would have been obliged to obey him. As for the Venetians, if we examine the course they followed, we see that they operated securely and gloriously as long as they fought with their own troops (this was before they started fighting on land); with their nobles and their common people armed, they fought courageously. But when they began to fight on land, they abandoned this successful strategy and followed the usual practices of waging war in Italy. As they first began to expand their territory on the mainland, since they did not have much territory there and enjoyed a high reputation, they had little to fear from their captains; but when their territory increased, which happened under Carmagnola,* the Venetians had a taste of this mistake; for, having found him very able, since under his command they had defeated the Duke of Milan, and knowing, on the other hand, that he had lost some of his fighting spirit, they judged that they could no longer conquer under him, for he had no wish to do so, yet they could not dismiss him for fear of losing what they had acquired; so in order to secure themselves against him, they were forced to execute him. Then they had as their captains Bartolomeo da Bergamo, Roberto da San Severino, the Count of Pitigliano,* and the like; with such as these they had to fear their losses, not their acquisitions, as occurred later at Vailà,* where, in a single day, they lost what had cost them eight hundred years of exhausting effort to acquire. From these soldiers, therefore, come only slow, tardy, and weak conquests and sudden and astonishing losses. And because with these examples I have begun to treat of Italy, which has for many years been ruled by mercenary soldiers, I should like to discuss the matter more thoroughly, in order that once their origin and developments are revealed they can be more easily corrected.

You must, then, understand how in recent times, when the Empire began to be driven out of Italy and the Pope began to win more prestige in temporal affairs, Italy was divided into many states; for many of the large cities took up arms against their nobles, who, at first backed by the Emperor, had kept them under their control; and the Church supported these cities to increase its temporal power; in many other cities citizens became princes. Hence, Italy having come almost entirely into the hands of the Church and of several republics, those priests and other citizens who were not accustomed to bearing arms began to hire foreigners. The first to give prestige to such troops was Alberigo of Conio,* a Romagnol. From this man's school emerged, among others, Braccio and Sforza, who in their day were the arbiters of Italy. After them came all the others who, until the present day, have commanded these soldiers. And the result of their ability has been that Italy has been overrun by Charles, plundered by Louis, violated by Ferdinand, and insulted by the Swiss. Their method was first to increase the reputation of their own forces by taking away the prestige of the infantry. They did so because they were men without a state of their own who lived by their profession; a small number of foot soldiers could not give them prestige, and they could not afford to hire a large number of them; and so they relied completely upon cavalry, since for having only a reasonable number of horsemen they were provided for and honoured. And they reduced things to such a state that in an army of twenty thousand troops, one could hardly find two thousand foot soldiers. Besides this, they had used every means to spare themselves and their soldiers hardship and fear, not killing each other in their battles but rather taking each other prisoner without demanding ransom; they would not attack cities at night; and those in the cities would not attack the tents of the besiegers; they built neither stockades nor trenches around their camps; they did not campaign in the winter. And all these things were permitted by their military code and gave them a means of escaping, as was stated, hardships and dangers: so that these condottieri have led Italy into slavery and humiliation.

CHAPTER XIII

On Auxiliary, Mixed, and Citizen Soldiers

AUXILIARY troops, the other kind of worthless armies, are those that arrive when you call a powerful man to bring his forces to your aid and defence, as was done in recent times by Pope Julius, who, having witnessed in the campaign of Ferrara the sad showing of his mercenary soldiers, turned to auxiliary soldiers and made an agreement with Ferdinand, King of Spain, that he assist him with his troops and his armies. These soldiers can be useful and good in themselves, but for the man who summons them they are almost always harmful; for, if they lose you are defeated; if they win you end up their prisoner. And although ancient histories are full of such instances, nevertheless I am unwilling to leave unexamined this recent example of Pope Julius II, whose policy could not have been more poorly considered, for, in wanting to take Ferrara, he threw himself completely into the hands of a foreigner. But his good fortune brought about a third development so that he did not gather the fruit of his poor decision: for after his auxiliaries were routed at Ravenna, the Swiss rose up and, to the consternation of Pope Julius as well as everyone else, chased out the victors. Thus, he was neither taken prisoner by his enemies, since they had fled, nor by his auxiliaries, since he triumphed with arms other than theirs. And the Florentines, completely unarmed, hired ten thousand French soldiers to take Pisa; such a plan endangered them more than any of their previous predicaments. The emperor of Constantinople,* in order to oppose his neighbours, brought ten thousand Turkish troops into Greece, who, when the war was over, did not want to leave; this was the beginning of Greek servitude under the infidel.

Anyone, therefore, who does not wish to conquer should make use of these soldiers, for they are much more dangerous than mercenary troops. Because with them defeat is certain: they are completely united and all under the command of others; but the mercenaries need more time and a greater opportunity if they are to harm you after they have been victorious, for they are not a united body and are hired and paid by you; a third party whom you may make their leader cannot immediately seize enough authority to harm you. In short, with mercenaries the greatest danger is their cowardice, with auxiliaries their courage.

A wise prince has always avoided these soldiers and has relied upon his own men; and he has chosen to lose with his own troops rather than to conquer with those of others, judging no true victory one gained by means of foreign armies. I shall never hesitate to cite Cesare Borgia and his deeds as an example. This Duke entered Romagna with auxiliary forces, leading an army composed entirely of Frenchmen; and with them he captured Imola and Forlì. But not thinking the troops reliable, he turned to mercenary forces, judging them to be less dangerous, and he hired the Orsini and Vitelli. When he found out that they were unreliable, unfaithful, and treacherous, he destroyed them and turned to his own men. And it is easy to see the difference between these two sorts of troops if we consider the difference between the Duke's reputation when he had only French troops and when he had the Orsini and Vitelli, as opposed to when he was left with his own troops and himself to depend on: we find that his reputation always increased; never was he esteemed more highly than when everyone saw that he was complete master of his own army.

I did not wish to depart from citing recent Italian examples; yet I do not want to omit Hiero of Syracuse, one of those I mentioned above. This man, as I said previously, having been named by the Syracusans captain of their armies, immediately realized that mercenary forces were useless, composed, as they were, of men resembling our own Italian condottieri; and it seemed to him that he could neither keep them on nor dismiss them, so he had them all cut to pieces: and afterwards he made war with his own troops and not with those of foreigners. I would also like to recall to mind an example from the Old Testament* that fits this argument. David offered himself to Saul to battle against Goliath, the Philistine challenger; Saul, in order to give him courage, armed him with his own armour, which David, when he had put it on, cast off, declaring that with it he could not test his true worth; he therefore wished to meet the enemy with his own sling and his own sword.

In short, the arms of another man either slide off your back, weigh you down, or tie you up. Charles VII, father of Louis XI, having freed France from the English by means of his good fortune and his ability, recognized the necessity of arming himself with his own men, and he set up in his kingdom an ordinance to procure cavalry and infantry. Later, his son, King Louis, abolished the ordinance of the infantry and began to hire Swiss troops; this mistake, followed by others as we can now witness, is the cause of the many threats to that kingdom. By giving prestige to the Swiss, he discredited his own troops; for he did away entirely with his foot soldiers and obliged his cavalry to depend upon the soldiers of others; being accustomed to fighting with the Swiss, the French horsemen felt that they could not conquer without them. From this it came about that the French were not strong enough to match the Swiss, and without the Swiss they did not dare to meet others. The armies of France have, therefore, been mixed, partly mercenaries and partly citizen troops; armies combined together in such a fashion are much better than a purely auxiliary force or a purely mercenary army, but are greatly inferior to one's own troops. And the example just cited should suffice, for the kingdom of France would be invincible if Charles's policy had been developed or retained. But man's shortsightedness will initiate a policy that seems good at the outset but does not notice the poison that is concealed underneath, as I said earlier* in connection with consumptive fevers.

And thus anyone who does not diagnose the ills when they arise in a principality is not really wise; and this skill is given to few men. And if the primary cause of the downfall of the Roman Empire is examined, one will find it to be only when the Goths began to be hired as mercenaries; because from that beginning the strength of the Roman Empire began to be weakened, and all that strength was drained from it and was given to the Goths.

I conclude, therefore, that without having one's own soldiers, no principality is safe; on the contrary, it is completely subject to fortune, not having the power and the loyalty to defend it in times of adversity. And it was always the opinion and belief of wise men that 'nothing is so unhealthy or unstable as the reputation for power that is not based upon one's own power.'* And one's own troops are those which are composed either of subjects or of citizens or your own dependants; all others are either mercenaries or auxiliaries. And the means to organize a citizen army are easily discovered if the methods followed by those four men I have cited above are examined, and if one observes how Philip, father of Alexander the Great, and many republics and princes have armed and organized themselves: in such methods I have full confidence.

CHAPTER XIV

A Prince's Duty Concerning Military Matters

A PRINCE, therefore, must not have any other object nor any other thought, nor must he take anything as his profession but war, its institutions, and its discipline; because that is the only profession which befits one who commands; and it is of such importance that not only does it maintain those who were born princes, but many times it enables men of private station to rise to that position; and, on the other hand, it is evident that when princes have given more thought to personal luxuries than to arms, they have lost their state. And the most important cause of losing it is to neglect this art; and the way to acquire it is to be well versed in this art.

Francesco Sforza became Duke of Milan from being a private citizen because he was armed; his successors, since they avoided the inconveniences of arms, became private citizens after having been dukes. For, among the other bad effects it causes, being unarmed makes you despised; this is one of those infamies a prince should guard himself against, as will be treated below:* for between an armed and an unarmed man there is no comparison whatsoever, and it is not reasonable for an armed man to obey an unarmed man willingly, nor that an unarmed man should be safe among armed servants; since, when the former is suspicious and the latter are contemptuous, it is impossible for them to work well together. And therefore, a prince who does not understand military matters, besides the other misfortunes already noted, cannot be esteemed by his own soldiers, nor can he trust them.

He should, therefore, never take his mind from this exercise of war, and in peacetime he must train himself more than in time of war; this can be done in two ways: one by action, the other by the mind. And as far as actions are concerned, besides keeping his soldiers well disciplined and trained, he must always be out hunting, and must accustom his body to hardships in this manner; and he must also learn the nature of the terrain, and know how mountains slope, how valleys open, how plains lie, and understand the nature of rivers and swamps; and he should devote much attention to such activities. Such knowledge is useful in two ways: first, one learns to know one's own country and can better understand how to defend it; second, with the knowledge and experience of the terrain, one can easily comprehend the characteristics of any other terrain that it is necessary to explore for the first time; for the hills, valleys, plains, rivers, and swamps of Tuscany, for instance, have certain similarities to those of other provinces; so that by knowing the lie of the land in one province one can easily understand it in others. And a prince who lacks this ability lacks the most important quality in a leader; because this skill teaches you to find the enemy, choose a campsite, lead troops, organize them for battle, and besiege towns to your own advantage.

Philopoemen,* Prince of the Achaeans, among the other praises given to him by writers, is praised because in peacetime he thought of nothing except the means of waging war; and when he was out in the country with his friends, he often stopped and reasoned with them: 'If the enemy were on that hilltop and we were here with our army, which of the two of us would have the advantage? How could we attack them without breaking formation? If we wanted to retreat, how could we do this? If they were to retreat, how could we pursue them?'

And he proposed to them, as they rode along, every predicament in which an army may find itself; he heard their opinions, expressed his own, and backed it up with arguments; so that, because of these continuous deliberations, when leading his troops no unforeseen incident could arise for which he did not have the remedy.

But as for the exercise of the mind, the prince must read histories and in them study the deeds of great men; he must see how they conducted themselves in wars; he must examine the reasons for their victories and for their defeats in order to avoid the latter and to imitate the former; and above all else he must do as some distinguished man before him has done, who elected to imitate someone who had been praised and honoured before him, and always keep in mind his deeds and actions; just as it is reported that Alexander the Great imitated Achilles; Caesar, Alexander; Scipio,* Cyrus. And anyone who reads the life of Cyrus* written by Xenophon will realize how important in the life of Scipio that imitation was for his glory and how much, in purity, goodness, humanity, and generosity, Scipio conformed to those characteristics of Cyrus that Xenophon had written about.

Such methods as these a wise prince must follow, and never in peaceful times must he be idle; but he must turn them diligently to his advantage in order to be able to profit from them in times of adversity, so that, when fortune changes, she will find him prepared to withstand such times.

CHAPTER XV

On Those Things for Which Men, and Particularly Princes, Are Praised or Blamed

Now there remains to be examined what should be the methods and procedures of a prince in dealing with his subjects and friends. And because I know that many have written about this, I am afraid that by writing about it again I shall be thought of as presumptuous, since in discussing this material

I depart radically from the procedures of others. But since my intention is to write something useful for anyone who understands it, it seemed more suitable to me to search after the effectual truth of the matter rather than its imagined one.* And many writers have imagined for themselves republics and principalities that have never been seen nor known to exist in reality; for there is such a gap between how one lives and how one ought to live that anyone who abandons what is done for what ought to be done learns his ruin rather than his preservation: for a man who wishes to profess goodness at all times will come to ruin among so many who are not good. Hence it is necessary for a prince who wishes to maintain his position to learn how not to be good, and to use this knowledge or not to use it according to necessity.

Leaving aside, therefore, the imagined things concerning a prince, and taking into account those that are true, I say that all men, when they are spoken of, and particularly princes, since they are placed on a higher level, are judged by some of these qualities which bring them either blame or praise. And this is why one is considered generous, another miserly (to use a Tuscan word, since 'avaricious' in our language is still used to mean one who wishes to acquire by means of theft; we call 'miserly' one who excessively avoids using what he has); one is considered a giver, the other rapacious; one cruel, another merciful; one treacherous, another faithful; one effeminate and cowardly, another bold and courageous; one humane, another haughty; one lascivious, another chaste; one trustworthy, another frivolous; one religious, another unbelieving; and the like. And I know that everyone will admit that it would be a very praiseworthy thing to find in a prince, of the qualities mentioned above, those that are held to be good; but since it is neither possible to have them nor to observe them all completely, because the human condition does not permit it, a prince must be prudent enough to know how to escape the bad reputation of those vices that would lose the state for him, and must protect himself from those that will not lose it for him, if this is possible; but if he cannot, he need not concern himself unduly if he ignores these less serious vices. And, moreover, he need not worry about incurring the bad reputation of those vices without which it would be difficult to hold his state; since, carefully taking everything into account, he will discover that something which appears to be a virtue, if pursued, will end in his destruction; while some other thing which seems to be a vice, if pursued, will result in his safety and his well-being.

CHAPTER XVI

On Generosity and Miserliness

BEGINNING, therefore, with the first of the above-mentioned qualities, I say that it would be good to be considered generous; nevertheless, generosity used in such a manner as to give you a reputation for it will harm you; because if it is employed virtuously and as one should employ it, it will not be recognized and you will not avoid the reproach of its opposite. And so, if a prince wants to maintain his reputation for generosity among men, it is necessary for him not to neglect any possible means of lavish display; in so doing such a prince will always use up all his resources and he will be obliged, eventually, if he wishes to maintain his reputation for generosity, to burden the people with excessive taxes and to do everything possible to raise funds. This will begin to make him hateful to his subjects, and, becoming impoverished, he will not be much esteemed by anyone; so that, as a consequence of his generosity, having offended many and rewarded few, he will feel the effects of any slight unrest and will be ruined at the first sign of danger; recognizing this and wishing to alter his policies, he immediately runs the risk of being reproached as a miser.

A prince, therefore, being unable to use this virtue of generosity in a manner which will not harm himself, if he is known for it, should, if he is wise, not worry about being called a miser; for with time he will come to be considered more generous once it is evident that, as a result of his parsimony, his income is sufficient, he can defend himself from anyone who makes war against him, and he can undertake enterprises without overburdening his people, so that he comes to be generous with all those from whom he takes nothing, who are countless, and miserly with all those to whom he gives nothing, who are few. In our times we have not seen great deeds accomplished except by those who were considered miserly; the others were failures. Pope Julius II, although he made use of his reputation for generosity in order to gain the papacy, then decided not to maintain it in order to be able to wage war; the present King of France has waged many wars without imposing extra taxes on his subjects, only because his habitual parsimony has provided for the additional expenditures; the present King of Spain, if he had been considered generous, would not have engaged in or won so many campaigns.

Therefore, in order not to have to rob his subjects, to be able to defend himself, not to become poor and contemptible, and not to be forced to become rapacious, a prince must consider it of little importance if he incurs the reputation of being a miser, for this is one of those vices that permits him to rule. And if someone were to say: Caesar with his generosity achieved imperial power, and many others, because they were generous and known to be so, achieved very high positions; I would reply: you are either already a prince or you are on the way to becoming one; in the first instance such generosity is damaging; in the second it is very necessary to be thought generous. And Caesar was one of those who wanted to gain the principality of Rome; but if, after obtaining this, he had lived and had not moderated his expenditures, he would have destroyed his rule. And if someone were to reply: there have existed many princes who have accomplished great deeds with their armies who have been reputed to be generous; I would answer you: a prince either spends his own money and that of his subjects or that of others; in the first case he must be economical; in the second he must not restrain any part of his generosity. And for that prince who goes out with his soldiers and lives by looting, sacking, and ransoms, who controls the property of others, such generosity is necessary; otherwise he would not be followed by his troops. And with what does not belong to you or to your subjects you can be a more liberal giver, as were Cyrus, Caesar, and Alexander; for spending the wealth of others does not lessen your reputation but adds to it;

only the spending of your own is what harms you. And there is nothing that uses itself up faster than generosity, for as you employ it you lose the means of employing it, and you become either poor and despised or else, in order to escape poverty, you become rapacious and hated. And above all other things a prince must guard himself against being despised and hated; and generosity leads you to both one and the other. So it is wiser to live with the reputation of a miser, which produces reproach without hatred, than to be forced to incur the reputation of rapacity, which produces reproach along with hatred, because you want to be considered generous.

CHAPTER XVII

On Cruelty and Mercy, and Whether It Is Better to Be Loved Than To Be Feared or the Contrary

PROCEEDING to the other qualities mentioned above, I say that every prince must desire to be considered merciful and not cruel; nevertheless, he must take care not to misuse this mercy. Cesare Borgia was considered cruel; none the less, his cruelty had brought order to Romagna, united it, restored it to peace and obedience. If we examine this carefully, we shall see that he was more merciful than the Florentine people, who, in order to avoid being considered cruel, allowed the destruction of Pistoia.* Therefore, a prince must not worry about the reproach of cruelty when it is a matter of keeping his subjects united and loyal; for with a very few examples of cruelty he will be more compassionate than those who, out of excessive mercy, permit disorders to continue, from which arise murders and plundering; for these usually harm the community at large, while the executions that come from the prince harm particular individuals. And the new prince, above all other princes, cannot escape the reputation of being called cruel, since new states are full of dangers. And Virgil, through Dido, states: 'My difficult condition and the newness of my rule make me act in such a manner, and to set guards over my land on all sides.'*

Nevertheless, a prince must be cautious in believing and in acting, nor should he be afraid of his own shadow; and he should proceed in such a manner, tempered by prudence and humanity, so that too much trust may not render him imprudent nor too much distrust render him intolerable.

From this arises an argument: whether it is better to be loved than to be feared, or the contrary. I reply that one should like to be both one and the other; but since it is difficult to join them together, it is much safer to be feared than to be loved when one of the two must be lacking. For one can generally say this about men: that they are ungrateful, fickle, simulators and deceivers, avoiders of danger, greedy for gain; and while you work for their good they are completely yours, offering you their blood, their property, their lives, and their sons, as I said earlier,* when danger is far away; but when it comes nearer to you they turn away. And that prince who bases his power entirely on their words, finding himself completely without other preparations, comes to ruin; for friendships that are acquired by a price and not by greatness and nobility of character are purchased but are not owned, and at the proper moment they cannot be spent. And men are less hesitant about harming someone who makes himself loved than one who makes himself feared because love is held together by a chain of obligation which, since men are wretched creatures, is broken on every occasion in which their own interests are concerned; but fear is sustained by a dread of punishment which will never abandon you.

A prince must nevertheless make himself feared in such a manner that he will avoid hatred, even if he does not acquire love; since to be feared and not to be hated can very well be combined; and this will always be so when he keeps his hands off the property and the women of his citizens and his subjects. And if he must take someone's life, he should do so when there is proper justification and manifest cause; but, above all, he should avoid seizing the property of others; for men forget more quickly the death of their father than the loss of their patrimony. Moreover, reasons for seizing their property are never lacking; and he who begins to live by stealing always finds a reason for taking what belongs to others; on the contrary, reasons for taking a life are rarer and disappear sooner.

But when the prince is with his armies and has under his command a multitude of troops, then it is absolutely necessary that he not worry about being considered cruel; for without that reputation he will never keep an army united or prepared for any combat. Among the praiseworthy deeds of Hannibal* is counted this: that, having a very large army, made up of all kinds of men, which he commanded in foreign lands, there never arose the slightest dissension, neither among themselves nor against their leader, both during his good and his bad fortune. This could not have arisen from anything other than his inhuman cruelty, which along with his many other qualities, made him always respected and terrifying in the eyes of his soldiers; and without that, to attain the same effect, his other qualities would not have sufficed. And the writers of history, having considered this matter very little, on the one hand admire these deeds of his and on the other condemn the main cause of them.

And that it is true that his other qualities would not have been sufficient can be seen from the example of Scipio, a most extraordinary man not only in his time but in all recorded history, whose armies in Spain rebelled against him; this came about from nothing other than his excessive compassion, which gave to his soldiers more liberty than military discipline allowed. For this he was censured in the senate by Fabius Maximus,* who called him the corruptor of the Roman militia. The Locrians, having been ruined by one of Scipio's officers, were not avenged by him, nor was the arrogance of that officer corrected, all because of his tolerant nature; so that someone in the senate who tried to apologize for him said that there were many men who knew how not to err better than they knew how to correct errors. Such a nature would have, in time, damaged Scipio's fame and glory if he had continued to command armies; but, living under the control of the senate, this harmful characteristic of his not only was concealed but brought him glory.

I conclude, therefore, returning to the problem of being feared and loved, that since men love at their own pleasure and fear at the pleasure of the prince, a wise prince should build his foundation upon that which belongs to him, not upon that which belongs to others: he must strive only to avoid hatred, as has been said.

CHAPTER XVIII

How a Prince Should Keep His Word

How praiseworthy it is for a prince to keep his word and to live by integrity and not by deceit everyone knows; nevertheless, one sees from the experience of our times that the princes who have accomplished great deeds are those who have cared little for keeping their promises and who have known how to manipulate the minds of men by shrewdness; and in the end they have surpassed those who laid their foundations upon loyalty.

You must, therefore, know that there are two means of fighting:* one according to the laws, the other with force; the first way is proper to man, the second to beasts; but because the first, in many cases, is not sufficient, it becomes necessary to have recourse to the second. Therefore, a prince must know how to use wisely the natures of the beast and the man. This policy was taught to princes allegorically by the ancient writers, who described how Achilles and many other ancient princes were given to Chiron the Centaur* to be raised and taught under his discipline. This can only mean that, having a half-beast and half-man as a teacher, a prince must know how to employ the nature of the one and the other; and the one without the other cannot endure.

Since, then, a prince must know how to make good use of the nature of the beast, he should choose from among the beasts the fox and the lion;* for the lion cannot defend itself from traps and the fox cannot protect itself from wolves. It is therefore necessary to be a fox in order to recognize the traps and a lion in order to frighten the wolves. Those who play only the part of the lion do not understand matters. A wise ruler, therefore, cannot and should not keep his word when such an observance of faith would be to his disadvantage and when the reasons which made him promise are removed. And if men were all good, this rule would not be good; but since men are a contemptible lot and will not keep their promises to you, you likewise need not keep yours to them. A prince never lacks legitimate reasons to break his promise. Of this one could cite an endless number of modern examples to show how many pacts, how many promises have been made null and void because of the infidelity of princes; and he who has known best how to use the fox has come to a better end. But it is necessary to know how to disguise this nature well and to be a great hypocrite and a liar: and men are so simple-minded and so controlled by their present needs that one who deceives will always find another who will allow himself to be deceived.

I do not wish to remain silent about one of these recent instances. Alexander VI did nothing else, he thought about nothing else, except to deceive men, and he always found the occasion to do this. And there never was a man who had more forcefulness in his oaths, who affirmed a thing with more promises, and who honoured his word less; nevertheless, his tricks always succeeded perfectly since he was well acquainted with this aspect of the world.

Therefore, it is not necessary for a prince to have all of the above-mentioned qualities, but it is very necessary for him to appear to have them. Furthermore, I shall be so bold as to assert this: that having them and practising them at all times is harmful; and appearing to have them is useful; for instance, to seem merciful, faithful, humane, trustworthy, religious, and to be so; but his mind should be disposed in such a way that should it become necessary not to be so, he will be able and know how to change to the contrary. And it is essential to understand this: that a prince, and especially a new prince, cannot observe all those things for which men are considered good, for in order to maintain the state he is often obliged to act against his promise, against charity, against humanity, and against religion. And therefore, it is necessary that he have a mind ready to turn itself according to the way the winds of fortune and the changeability of affairs require him; and, as

I said above, as long as it is possible, he should not stray from the good, but he should know how to enter into evil when necessity commands.

A prince, therefore, must be very careful never to let anything slip from his lips which is not full of the five qualities mentioned above: he should appear, upon seeing and hearing him, to be all mercy, all faithfulness, all integrity, all kindness, all religion. And there is nothing more necessary than to seem to possess this last quality. And men in general judge more by their eyes than their hands; for everyone can see but few can feel. Everyone sees what you seem to be, few touch upon what you are, and those few do not dare to contradict the opinion of the many who have the majesty of the state to defend them; and in the actions of all men, and especially of princes, where there is no impartial arbiter, one must consider the final result.* Let a prince therefore act to conquer and to maintain the state; his methods will always be judged honourable and will be praised by all; for ordinary people are always deceived by appearances and by the outcome of a thing; and in the world there is nothing but ordinary people; and there is no room for the few, while the many have a place to lean on. A certain prince of the present day,* whom I shall refrain from naming, preaches nothing but peace and faith, and to both one and the other he is entirely opposed; and both, if he had put them into practice, would have cost him many times over either his reputation or his state.

CHAPTER XIX

On Avoiding Being Despised and Hated

But now that I have talked about the most important of the qualities mentioned above, I would like to discuss the others briefly in this general manner: that the prince, as was noted above, should concentrate upon avoiding those things which make him hated and despised; and when he has avoided this, he will have carried out his duties and will find no danger whatsoever in other vices. As I have said, what makes him hated above all else is being rapacious and a usurper of the property and the women of his subjects; he must refrain from this; and in most cases, so long as you do not deprive them of either their property or their honour, the majority of men live happily; and you have only to deal with the ambition of a few, who can be restrained without difficulty and by many means. What makes him despised is being considered changeable, frivolous, effeminate, cowardly, irresolute; from these qualities a prince must guard himself as if from a reef, and he must strive to make everyone recognize in his actions greatness, spirit, dignity, and strength; and concerning the private affairs of his subjects, he must insist that his decision be irrevocable; and he should maintain himself in such a way that no man could imagine that he can deceive or cheat him.

That prince who projects such an opinion of himself is greatly esteemed; and it is difficult to conspire against a man with such a reputation and difficult to attack him, provided that he is understood to be of great merit and revered by his subjects. For a prince should have two fears: one, internal, concerning his subjects; the other, external, concerning foreign powers. From the latter he can defend himself by his good troops and friends; and he will always have good friends if he has good troops; and internal affairs will always be stable when external affairs are stable, provided that they are not already disturbed by a conspiracy; and even if external conditions change, if he is properly organized and lives as I have said and does not lose control of himself, he will always be able to withstand every attack, just as I said that Nabis the Spartan did. But concerning his subjects, when external affairs do not change, he has to fear that they may conspire secretly: the prince secures himself from this by avoiding being hated or despised and by keeping the people satisfied with him; this is a necessary accomplishment, as was treated above at length. And one of the most powerful remedies a prince has against conspiracies is not to be hated by the masses; for a man who plans a conspiracy always believes that he will satisfy the people by killing the prince; but when he thinks he might anger them, he cannot work up the courage to undertake such a deed; for the problems on the side of the conspirators are countless. And experience demonstrates that there have been many conspiracies but few have been concluded successfully; for anyone who conspires cannot be alone, nor can he find companions except from amongst those whom he believes to be dissatisfied; and as soon as you have revealed your intention to one malcontent, you give him the means to make himself content, since he can have everything he desires by uncovering the plot; so much is this so that, seeing a sure gain on the one hand and one doubtful and full of danger on the other, if he is to maintain faith with you he has to be either an unusually good friend or a completely determined enemy of the prince. And to treat the matter briefly, I say that on the part of the conspirator there is nothing but fear, jealousy, and the thought of punishment that terrifies him; but on the part of the prince there is the majesty of the principality, the laws, the defences of friends and the state to protect him; so that, with the good will of the people added to all these things, it is impossible for anyone to be so rash as to plot against him. For, where usually a conspirator has to be afraid before he executes his evil deed, in this case he must be afraid even after the crime is performed, having the people as an enemy, nor can he hope to find any refuge because of this.

One could cite countless examples on this subject; but I shall be satisfied with only the one which occurred during the time of our fathers. Messer Annibale Bentivogli,* prince of Bologna and grandfather of the present Messer Annibale, was murdered by the Canneschi family, who conspired against him; he left behind no heir except Messer Giovanni, then only a baby. As soon as this murder occurred, the people rose up and killed all the Canneschi. This came about because of the good will that the house of the Bentivogli enjoyed in those days; this good will was so great that with Annibale dead, and there being no one of that family left in the city who could rule Bologna, the Bolognese people, having heard that in Florence there was one of the Bentivogli blood who was believed until that time to be the son of a blacksmith, went to Florence to find him, and they gave him the control of that city; it was ruled by him until Messer Giovanni became of age to rule.

I conclude, therefore, that a prince should not be too concerned with conspiracies when the people are well disposed toward him; but when the populace is hostile and regards him with hatred, he must fear everything and everyone. And well-organized states and wise princes have, with great diligence, taken care not to anger the nobles and to satisfy the common people and keep them contented; for this is one of the most important concerns that a prince has.

Among the kingdoms in our times that are well organized and well governed is that of France: in it one finds countless good institutions upon which depend the liberty and the security of the king; of these the foremost is the parliament and its authority. For he who organized that kingdom, recognizing the ambition of the nobles and their insolence, and being aware of the necessity of keeping a bit in their mouths to hold them back, on the one hand, while, on the other, knowing the hatred, based upon fear, of the populace for the nobles, and wanting to reassure them, did not wish this to be the particular obligation of the king. In order to relieve himself of the difficulties he might incur from the nobles if he supported the common people, and from the common people if he supported the nobles, he established a third judicial body that might restrain the nobles and favour the masses without burdening the king. There could be no better nor more prudent an institution than this, nor could there be a better reason for the safety of the king and the kingdom. From this one can extract another notable observation: that princes must delegate distasteful tasks to others; pleasant ones they should keep for themselves. Again I conclude that a prince must respect the nobles but not make himself hated by the common people.

Perhaps it may seem to many who have studied the lives and deaths of some Roman emperors that they afford examples contrary to my point of view; for we find that some of them always lived nobly and demonstrated great strength of character yet nevertheless lost their empire or were killed by their own subjects who plotted against them. Wishing, therefore, to reply to these objections, I shall discuss the traits of several emperors, showing the reasons for their ruin, which are not different from those which I myself have already deduced; and I shall bring forward for consideration those things which are worthy of note for anyone who reads about the history of those times. And I shall let it suffice to choose all those emperors who succeeded to the throne from Marcus the philosopher to Maximinus: these were Marcus, his son Commodus, Pertinax, Julian, Severus, Antoninus Caracalla his son, Macrinus, Heliogabalus, Alexander, and Maximinus.* And it is first to be noted that while in other principalities one has only to contend with the ambition of the nobles and the arrogance of the people, the Roman emperors had a third problem: they had to endure the cruelty and the avarice of the soldiers. This created such difficulties that it was the cause of the downfall of many of them, since it was hard to satisfy both the soldiers and the populace; for the people loved peace and quiet and because of this loved modest princes, while the soldiers loved the prince who had a military character and who was arrogant, cruel, and rapacious; they wanted him to practise such qualities on the people so that they might double their pay and give vent to their avarice and cruelty. As a result of this situation, those emperors always came to ruin who by nature or by guile did not have so great a reputation that they could keep both the people and the soldiers in check; and most of them, especially those who came to power as new princes, recognizing the difficulty resulting from these two opposing factions, turned to appeasing the soldiers, caring little about injuring the people. Such a decision was necessary; since princes cannot avoid being hated by somebody, they must first seek not to be hated by the bulk of the populace; and when they cannot achieve this, they must try with every effort to avoid the hatred of the most powerful group. And therefore, those emperors who had need of extraordinary support because of their newness in power allied themselves with the soldiers instead of the people; nevertheless, this proved to their advantage or not, according to whether the prince knew how to maintain his reputation with the soldiers.

For the reasons listed above, it came about that, of Marcus, Pertinax, and Alexander, all of whom lived modest lives, were lovers of justice, enemies of cruelty, humane, and kindly, all except Marcus came to an unhappy end. Marcus alone lived and died with the greatest of honour, for he succeeded to the empire by birthright, and he did not have to recognize any obligation for it either to the soldiers or to the people; then, being endowed with many characteristics which made him revered, he always held, while he was alive, both the one party and the other within their limits, and he was never either hated or despised. But Pertinax was made emperor against the will of the soldiers, who, being used to living licentiously under Commodus, could not tolerate the righteous manner of life to which Pertinax wished to return them; whereupon, having made himself hated, and since to this hatred was added contempt for his old age, he came to ruin at the initial stage of his rule.

And here one must note that hatred is acquired just as much by means of good actions as by bad ones; and so, as I said above, if a prince wishes to maintain the state, he is often obliged not to be good; because whenever that group which you believe you need to support you is corrupted, whether it be the common people, the soldiers, or the nobles, it is to your advantage to follow their inclinations in order to satisfy them; and then good actions are your enemy. But let us come to Alexander. He was of such goodness that among the other laudable deeds attributed to him is this: in the fourteen years that he ruled the empire he never put anyone to death without a trial; nevertheless, since he was considered effeminate and a man who let himself be ruled by his mother, because of this he was despised, and the army plotted against him and murdered him.

Considering now, in contrast, the characteristics of Commodus, Severus, Antoninus Caracalla, and Maximinus, you will find them extremely cruel and greedy: in order to satisfy their troops, they did not hesitate to inflict all kinds of injuries upon the people; and all except Severus came to a sorry end. For in Severus there was so much ability that, keeping the soldiers as his friends even though the people were oppressed by him, he was always able to rule happily; for those qualities of his made him so esteemed in the eyes of both the soldiers and the common people that the former were awestruck and stupefied and the latter were respectful and satisfied.

And since the actions of this man were great and noteworthy

for a new prince, I wish to demonstrate briefly how well he knew how to use the masks of the fox and the lion, whose natures, as I say above, a prince must imitate. As soon as Severus learned of the indecisiveness of the emperor Julian, he convinced the army of which he was in command in Slavonia that it would be a good idea to march to Rome to avenge the death of Pertinax, who had been murdered by the Praetorian Guards. And under this pretext, without showing his desire to rule the empire, he moved his army to Rome, and he was in Italy before his departure was known. When he arrived in Rome, the senate, out of fear, elected him emperor, and Julian was killed. After this beginning, there remained two obstacles for Severus if he wanted to make himself master of the whole state: the first in Asia, where Pescennius Niger, commander of the Asiatic armies, had himself named emperor; and the other in the West, where Albinus was, who also aspired to the empire. And since he judged it dangerous to reveal himself as an enemy to both of them, he decided to attack Niger and to deceive Albinus. He wrote to the latter that, having been elected emperor by the senate, he wanted to share that honour with him; and he sent him the title of Caesar and, by decree of the senate, he made him his coequal: these things were accepted by Albinus as the truth. But after Severus had conquered and executed Niger and had pacified affairs in the East, upon returning to Rome, he complained to the senate that Albinus, ungrateful for the benefits received from him, had treacherously sought to kill him, and for this he was obliged to go and punish his ingratitude. Then he went to find him in France and took both his state and his life.

Anyone, therefore, who will carefully examine the actions of this man will find him a very ferocious lion and a very shrewd fox; and he will see him feared and respected by everyone and not hated by his armies; and one should not be amazed that he, a new man, was able to hold so great an empire; for his outstanding reputation always defended him from that hatred which the common people could have had for him on account of his plundering. But Antoninus, his son, was also a man who had excellent abilities which made him greatly admired in the eyes of the people and pleasing to the soldiers, for he was a military man, most able to support any kind of hardship, a despiser of all delicate foods and soft living; this made him loved by all the armies; nevertheless, his ferocity and cruelty were so great and so unusual – since he had, after countless individual killings, put to death a large part of the populace of Rome and all that of Alexandria – that he became most despised all over the world. And he aroused the fears even of those whom he had around him, so that he was murdered by a centurion in the midst of his army. From this it is to be noted that such deaths as these, which result from the deliberation of a determined individual, are unavoidable for princes, since anyone who does not fear death can harm them; but the prince must not be too afraid of such men, for they are very rare. He must only guard against inflicting serious injury on anyone who serves him and anyone he has about him in the administration of the principality: Antoninus had done this, for he had shamefully put to death a brother of that centurion, and he threatened the man every day; yet he kept him as a bodyguard. This was a rash decision and, as it happened, one which would bring about his downfall.

But let us come to Commodus, who held the empire with great ease, having inherited it by birth, being the son of Marcus; and it would have been enough for him to follow in the footsteps of his father in order to satisfy the soldiers and the common people. But being a cruel and bestial person by nature, in order to practise his greed upon the common people, he turned to pleasing the armies and to making them undisciplined; on the other hand, by not maintaining his dignity, frequently descending into the arenas to fight with the gladiators and doing other degrading things unworthy of the imperial majesty, he became contemptible in the sight of the soldiers. And being hated on the one hand, and despised on the other, he was plotted against and murdered.

The qualities of Maximinus remain to be described. He was a very warlike man; and because the armies were angered by Alexander's softness, which I explained above, after Alexander's death they elected him to the empire. He did not retain it very long, for two things made him hated and despised: the first was his base origin, having herded sheep once in Thrace (this fact was well known everywhere and it caused him to lose considerable dignity in everyone's eyes); the second was that at the beginning of his reign he deferred going to Rome to take possession of the imperial throne, and he had acquired the reputation of being very cruel, having through his prefects, in Rome and in all other parts of the empire, committed many cruelties. As a result, the entire world was moved by disgust for his ignoble birth and by the hatred brought about by fear of his cruelty; first Africa revolted, then the senate with the entire populace of Rome, and finally all of Italy conspired against him. To this was added even his own army; for, while besieging Aquileia and finding the capture difficult, angered by his cruelty and fearing him less, seeing that he had many enemies, they murdered him.

I do not wish to discuss Heliogabalus or Macrinus or Julian, who, since they were universally despised, were immediately disposed of; but I shall come to the conclusion of this discourse. And I say that the princes of our times in their affairs suffer less from this problem of satisfying their soldiers by extraordinary means, for, although they have to consider them to some extent, yet they resolve the question quickly, for none of these princes has standing armies which have evolved along with the government and the administration of the provinces as did the armies of the Roman empire. And therefore, if it was then necessary to satisfy the soldiers more than the common people, it was because the soldiers could do more than the common people; now it is more necessary for all princes, except the Turk and the Sultan,* to satisfy the common people more than the soldiers, since the people can do more than the soldiers. I make an exception of the Turk, for he always maintains near him twelve thousand infantrymen and fifteen thousand cavalrymen, upon whom depend the safety and the strength of his kingdom, and it is necessary that, setting aside all other concerns, that ruler maintain them as his friends. Likewise, the kingdom of the Sultan being entirely in the hands of the soldiers, it is fitting that he, too, should maintain them as his friends without respect to the people. And you must note that this state of the Sultan is unlike all the other principalities, since it is similar to the Christian pontificate, which cannot be called either a hereditary principality or a new principality; for it is not the sons of the old prince that are the heirs and that remain as lords, but instead the one who is elected to that rank by those who have the authority to do so. And because this system is an ancient one, it cannot be called a new principality, for in it are none of these difficulties that are to be found in new ones, since, although the prince is new, the institutions of that state are old and are organized to receive him as if he were their hereditary ruler.

But let us return to our subject. Let me say that anyone who considers the discourse written above will see how either hatred or contempt has been the cause of the ruin of these previously mentioned emperors; and he will also recognize how it comes to pass that, although some acted in one way and others in a contrary manner, in each of these groups one man had a happy end and the others an unhappy one. Because for Pertinax and Alexander, being new princes, it was useless and damaging to wish to imitate Marcus, who was installed in the principality by hereditary right; and likewise for Caracalla, Commodus, and Maximinus, it was disastrous to imitate Severus, since they did not have enough ability to follow in his footsteps. Therefore, a new prince in a new principality cannot imitate the deeds of Marcus, nor yet does he need to follow those of Severus; instead, he should take from Severus those attributes which are necessary to found his state and from Marcus those which are suitable and glorious in order to conserve a state which is already established and stable.

CHAPTER XX

On Whether Fortresses and Many Things that Princes Employ Every Day Are Useful or Harmful

SOME princes have disarmed their subjects in order to hold the state securely; others have kept their conquered lands divided; some have encouraged hostilities against themselves; others have turned to winning the support of those who were suspect at the beginning of their rule; some have built fortresses; others have torn them down and destroyed them. And although one cannot give a definite rule concerning these matters without knowing the particular details of those states wherein one had to take some similar decision, nevertheless I shall speak in as general a manner as the subject matter will allow.

Now there has never been a time when a new prince disarmed his subjects; on the contrary, when he has found them unarmed he has always armed them, because when armed those arms become yours; those whom you suspect become faithful, and those who were faithful remain so, and they become your partisans rather than your subjects. And since all of your subjects cannot be armed, when those you arm are favoured you can deal more securely with the others; and that distinction in treatment which they recognize toward themselves makes them obliged to you; the others excuse you, judging it necessary that those who are in more danger and who hold more responsibility should have more reward. But when you disarm them you begin to offend them; you demonstrate that you have no trust in them, either out of cowardice or from little confidence in them; and both these attitudes generate hatred against you. And since you cannot be unarmed, you will have to turn to mercenary soldiers, who have the characteristics explained above; and even if they were good, they could not be strong enough to defend you from powerful enemies and from unfaithful subjects. Therefore, as I have said, a new prince in a new principality has always instituted an army; and history is full of such examples.

But when a prince acquires a new state that, like a member, is joined to his old one, then it is necessary to disarm that state, except for those who have been your partisans in its acquisition; and they as well, with time and the appropriate opportunity, must be rendered weak and effeminate; and things must be organized in such a fashion that the armed strength of your entire state will be concentrated in your own troops who live near to you in your older state.

Our ancestors, and those who were considered wise, used to say that it was necessary to hold Pistoia by factions and Pisa by fortresses; and because of this they would encourage factional strife in some of their subject towns in order to control them more easily. This advice, during those times when Italy had, to a certain extent, a balance of power, may have been a good policy; but I do not believe that today it can be given as a rule, since I do not think that factions ever did any good. On the contrary, when the enemy approaches, divided cities are, of necessity, always lost; for the weaker factions will always join the external forces and the others will not be able to resist.

The Venetians, moved by the reasons stated above, I believe, encouraged the Guelf and Ghibelline factions* in their subject cities; and although they never permitted matters to come to bloodshed, they still fostered these quarrels between them so that those citizens, busy with their own disputes, would not unite against them. This, as we have seen, did not result in their gain; for, having been defeated at Vailà, one faction of these cities immediately took courage and seized the entire territory from them. Methods such as these, moreover, imply weakness in a prince; for in a strong principality such divisions will never be allowed, since they are profitable only in peace-time, allowing the subjects to be more easily controlled by such means; but when war comes such a policy reveals its defects.

Without a doubt, princes become great when they overcome difficulties and obstacles that are imposed on them; and therefore fortune, especially when she wishes to increase the reputation of a new prince, who has a greater need to acquire prestige than a hereditary prince does, creates enemies for him and has them take action against him so that he will have the chance to overcome them and to climb higher up the ladder his enemies have brought him. Therefore many judge that a wise prince must, whenever he has the occasion, foster with cunning some hostility so that in stamping it out his greatness will increase as a result.

Princes, and especially those who are new, have discovered more loyalty and more utility in those men who, at the beginning of their rule, were considered suspect than in those who were at first trusted. Pandolfo Petrucci,* prince of Siena, ruled his state more with the assistance of men who had been held in suspicion than by others. But on this issue one cannot speak in generalities, for it varies according to the case. I shall only say this: that the prince will always easily win the support of those men who had been enemies at the start of a principality, the kind who must have support in order to maintain themselves; and they are even more obliged to serve him faithfully inasmuch as they recognize the need, through their actions, to cancel the suspicious opinion that the prince had of them. And thus, the prince will always derive more profit from them than from those who, serving him with too much security, neglect his affairs.

And since the subject requires it, I do not wish to fail to remind princes who have conquered a state recently by means of assistance from its inhabitants to consider carefully what cause may have moved those who have helped him to do so; and if it is not natural affection for him, but simply because they were not happy with the preceding state, he will be able to keep them as his allies only with hard work and the greatest of difficulty, since it will be impossible for him to satisfy them. And considering carefully the reason for this, with the examples taken from antiquity and from modern times, it will be seen that he can more easily win friends for himself from among those men who were content with the preceding state, and therefore were his enemies, than from those who, since they were not satisfied with it, became his allies and helped him to occupy it.

In order to hold their states more securely, princes have been accustomed to build fortresses that may serve as the bridle and bit for those who might plot an attack against them, and to have a secure shelter from a sudden rebellion. I praise this method, because it has been used since ancient times; nevertheless, Messer Niccolò Vitelli,* in our own times, was seen to demolish two fortresses in Città di Castello in order to hold that state; Guido Ubaldo,* Duke of Urbino, on returning to the rule from which Cesare Borgia had driven him, completely destroyed all the fortresses of that province, and he decided that without them it would be more difficult to recapture that state; the Bentivogli,* having returned to power in Bologna, took similar measures. Fortresses, then, are either useful or not, according to the circumstances: if they benefit you in one way they injure you in another. This matter may be dealt with as follows: that prince who is more afraid of his own people than of foreigners should build fortresses; but one who is more afraid of foreigners than of his people should not consider constructing them. The castle of Milan, which Francesco Sforza built there, has caused and will cause more wars against the Sforza family than any other disorder in that state. However, the best fortress that exists is not to be hated by the people; because, although you may have fortresses, they will not save you if the people hate you; for once the people have taken up arms, they never lack for foreigners who will aid them. In our times we have not seen that they have benefited any prince except the Countess of Forlì* after her husband, Count Girolamo, was killed; for because of her castle she was able to escape the popular uprising and to wait until help arrived from Milan in order to regain her state. And the times were such at that moment that no foreigner could give assistance to her people. But then fortresses were of little use to her when Cesare Borgia attacked her and when her hostile populace joined with the foreigner. Therefore, then and earlier, it would have been safer for her not to have been hated by her people than to have had the fortresses.

Considering all these matters, therefore, I praise both those princes who build fortresses and those who do not; and I criticize any prince who, trusting in fortresses, considers the hatred of the people to be of little importance.

CHAPTER XXI

How a Prince Should Act to Acquire Esteem

NOTHING makes a prince more esteemed than great undertakings and examples of his unusual talents. In our own times we have Ferdinand of Aragon, the present King of Spain. This man can be called almost a new prince, since from being a weak ruler he became, through fame and glory, the first king of Christendom; and if you consider his accomplishments, you will find them all very grand and some even extraordinary.

In the beginning of his reign he attacked Granada, and that enterprise was the basis of his state. First, he acted while things were peaceful and when he had no fear of opposition: he kept the minds of the barons of Castile busy with this, and they, concentrating on that war, did not consider changes at home. And he acquired, through that means, reputation and power over them without their noticing it; he was able to maintain armies with money from the Church and the people, and with that long war he laid a basis for his own army, which has since brought him honour. Besides this, in order to be able to undertake greater enterprises, always using religion for his own purposes, he turned to a pious cruelty, hunting down and clearing out the Moors from his kingdom: no example could be more pathetic or more unusual than this. He attacked Africa, under the same cloak of religion; he undertook the invasion of Italy; he finally attacked France. And in such a manner, he has always done and planned great deeds which have always kept the minds of his subjects in suspense and amazed and occupied with their outcome. And one action of his would spring from another in such a way that between one and the other he would never give men enough time to be able to work calmly against him.

It also helps a prince a great deal to display rare examples of his skills in dealing with internal affairs, such as those which are reported about Messer Bernabò Visconti* of Milan. When the occasion arises that a person in public life performs some extraordinary act, be it good or evil, he should find a way of rewarding or punishing him that will provoke a great deal of discussion. And above all, a prince should strive in all of his deeds to give the impression of a great man of superior intelligence.

A prince is also respected when he is a true friend and a true enemy; that is, when he declares himself on the side of one prince against another without any reservation. Such a policy will always be more useful than that of neutrality; for if two powerful neighbours of yours come to blows, they will be of the type that, when one has emerged victorious, you will either have cause to fear the victor or you will not. In either of these two cases, it will always be more useful for you to declare yourself and to fight an open war; for, in the first case, if you do not declare your intentions, you will always be the prey of the victor to the delight and satisfaction of the vanquished, and you will have no reason why anyone would come to your assistance; because whoever wins does not want reluctant allies who would not assist him in times of adversity; and whoever loses will not give you refuge since you were unwilling to run the risk of coming to his aid.

Antiochus came into Greece, sent there by the Aetolians to drive out the Romans. Antiochus sent envoys to the Achaeans, who were friends of the Romans, to encourage them to adopt a neutral policy; and, on the other hand, the Romans were urging them to take up arms on their behalf. This matter came up for debate in the council of the Achaeans, where the legate of Antiochus persuaded them to remain neutral; to this the Roman legate replied: 'The counsel these men give you about not entering the war is indeed contrary to your interests; without respect, without dignity, you will be the prey of the victors.'

And it will always happen that he who is not your friend will request your neutrality and he who is your friend will ask you to declare yourself by taking up your arms. And irresolute princes, in order to avoid present dangers, follow the neutral road most of the time, and most of the time they are ruined. But when the prince declares himself vigorously in favour of one side, if the one with whom you have joined wins, although he may be powerful and you may be left to his discretion, he has an obligation to you and there does exist a bond of friendship; and men are never so dishonest that they will crush you with such a show of ingratitude; and then, victories are never so clear-cut that the victor need be completely free of caution, especially when justice is concerned. But if the one with whom you join loses, you will be taken in by him; and while he is able, he will help you, and you will become the comrade of a fortune which can rise up again.

In the second case, when those who fight together are of such a kind that you need not fear the one who wins, it is even more prudent to join his side, since you go to the downfall of a prince with the aid of another prince who should have saved him if he had been wise; and in winning he is at your discretion, and it is impossible for him not to win with your aid.

And here it is to be noted that a prince should avoid ever joining forces with one more powerful than himself against others unless necessity compels it, as was said above; for you remain his prisoner if you win, and princes should avoid, as much as possible, being left at the mercy of others. The Venetians allied themselves with France against the Duke of Milan; and they could have avoided that alliance, which resulted in their ruin. But when such an alliance cannot be avoided (as happened to the Florentines when the Pope and Spain led their armies to attack Lombardy), then a prince should join in, for the reasons given above. Nor should any state ever believe that it can always choose safe courses of action; on the contrary, it should think that they will all be doubtful; for we find this to be in the order of things: that we never try to avoid one disadvantage without running into another; but prudence consists in knowing how to recognize the nature of disadvantages and how to choose the least bad as good.

A prince also should demonstrate that he is a lover of talent by giving recognition to men of ability and by honouring those who excel in a particular field. Furthermore, he should encourage his subjects to be free to pursue their trades in tranquillity, whether in commerce, agriculture, or in any other trade a man may have. And he should act in such a way that a man is not afraid to increase his goods for fear that they will be taken away from him, while another will not be afraid to engage in commerce for fear of taxes; instead, he must set up rewards for those who wish to do these things, and for anyone who seeks in any way to aggrandize his city or state. He should, besides this, at the appropriate times of the year, keep the populace occupied with festivals and spectacles. And because each city is divided into guilds or clans, he should take account of these groups, meet with them on occasion, offer himself as an example of humanity and munificence, always, nevertheless, maintaining firmly the dignity of his position, for this should never be lacking in any way.

CHAPTER XXII

On the Prince's Private Advisers

THE choice of advisers is of no little import to a prince; and they are good or not, according to the wisdom of the prince. The first thing one does to evaluate the wisdom of a ruler is to examine the men that he has around him; and when they are capable and faithful one can always consider him wise, for he has known how to recognize their ability and to keep them loyal; but when they are otherwise one can always form a low impression of him; for the first error he makes is made in this choice of advisers.

There was no one who knew Messer Antonio da Venafro,* adviser of Pandolfo Petrucci, Prince of Siena, who did not judge Pandolfo to be a very worthy man for having him as his minister. For there are three types of intelligence: one understands on its own, the second discerns what others understand, the third neither understands by itself nor through the intelligence of others; that first kind is most excellent, the second excellent, the third useless; therefore, it was necessary that if Pandolfo's intelligence were not of the first sort it must have been of the second: for, whenever a man has the intelligence to recognize the good or the evil that a man does or says, although he may not have original ideas of his own, he recognizes the bad deeds and the good deeds of the adviser, and he is able to praise the latter and to correct the others; and the adviser cannot hope to deceive him and thus he maintains his good behaviour.

But as to how a prince may know the adviser, there is this way which never fails. When you see that the adviser thinks more about himself than about you, and that in all his deeds he seeks his own interests, such a man as this will never be a good adviser and you will never be able to trust him; for a man who has the state of another in his hand must never think about himself but always about his prince, and he must never be concerned with anything that does not concern his prince.

And on the other hand, the prince should think of the adviser in order to keep him good – honouring him, making him wealthy, putting him in his debt, giving him a share of the honours and the responsibilities – so that the adviser sees that he cannot exist without the prince and so his abundant wealth will not make him desire more riches, or his many duties make him fear changes. When, therefore, advisers and princes are of such a nature in their dealings with each other, they can have faith in each other; and when they are otherwise, the outcome will always be harmful either to the one or to the other.

CHAPTER XXIII

On How to Avoid Flatterers

I DO not wish to omit an important matter and an error from which princes protect themselves with difficulty if they are not very clever or if they do not have good judgement. And these are the flatterers which fill the courts; for men delight so much in their own concerns, deceiving themselves in this manner, that they protect themselves from this plague with difficulty; and wishing to defend oneself from them brings with it the danger of becoming despised. For there is no other way to guard yourself against flattery than by making men understand that telling you the truth will not offend you; but when each man is able to tell you the truth you lose their respect. Therefore, a wise prince should take a third course, choosing wise men for his state and giving only those free rein to speak the truth to him, and only on such matters as he inquires about and not on others. But he should ask them about everything and should hear their opinions, and afterwards he should deliberate by himself in his own way; and with these counsels and with each of his advisers he should conduct himself in such a manner that all will realize that the more freely they speak the more they will be acceptable to him; besides these things, he should not want to hear any others, he should follow through on the policy decided upon, and he should be firm in his decisions. Anyone who does otherwise is either prey for flatterers or changes his mind often with the variance of opinions: because of this he is not respected.

I wish, in this regard, to cite a modern example. Father Luca,* the representative of the present Emperor Maximilian, explained, speaking about His Majesty, how the emperor never sought advice from anyone, nor did he ever do anything in his own way; this came about because of the emperor's secretive nature, a policy contrary to the one discussed above. He communicates his plans to no one, he accepts no advice about them; but as they begin to be recognized and discovered as they are put into effect, they begin to be criticized by those around him; and he, being easily influenced, is drawn away from his plans. From this results the fact that those things he achieves in one day he destroys during the next, and no one ever understands what he wishes or plans to do, and one cannot rely upon his decisions.

A prince, therefore, should always seek counsel, but when he wishes and not when others wish it; on the contrary, he should discourage anyone from giving him counsel unless it is requested. But he should be a great inquisitor and then, concerning the matters inquired about, a patient listener to the truth; furthermore, if he learns that anyone, for any reason, does not tell him the truth, he should become angry. And although many feel that any prince who is considered clever is so reputed not because of his own character but because of the good advisers he has around him, without a doubt they are deceived. For this is a general rule which never fails: that a prince who is not wise in his own right cannot be well advised, unless by chance he has submitted himself to a single person who governs him in everything and who is a very prudent individual. In this case he could well receive good advice, but it would not last long because that adviser would in a brief time take the state away from him. But if he seeks advice from more than one, a prince who is not wise will never have consistent advice, nor will he know how to make it consistent on his own; each of his advisers will think about his own interests; he will not know either how to correct or to understand them. And one cannot find advisers who are otherwise, for men always turn out badly for you unless some necessity makes them good. Therefore, it is to be concluded that good advice, from whomever it may come, must arise from the prudence of the prince and not the prince's prudence from the good advice.

CHAPTER XXIV

Why Italian Princes Have Lost Their States

THE things written above, if followed prudently, make a new prince seem well established and render him immediately safer and more established in his state than if he had been in it for some time. For a new prince is far more closely observed in his activities than is a hereditary prince; and when his deeds are recognized to be good actions they attract men much more and bind them to him more strongly than does antiquity of lineage. For men are much more taken by present concerns than by those of the past; and when they find the present satisfactory they enjoy it and seek nothing more; in fact, they will seize every measure to defend the new prince as long as he is not lacking in his other responsibilities. And thus he will have a double glory: that of having given birth to a new principality and of having adorned it and strengthened it with good laws, good arms, and good examples; as he will have double shame who, having been born a prince, loses his principality on account of his lack of prudence.

And if one considers those rulers in Italy that have lost their states in our times, such as the King of Naples, the Duke of Milan, and others, one discovers in them, first, a common defect in so far as arms are concerned, for the reasons that were discussed at length earlier; and then, one sees that some had the people hostile to them, while others had the people well disposed towards them but were unable to control the nobles; for without these defects states are not lost which have enough strength to take an army into battle. Philip of Macedonia* – not the father of Alexander but the one who was defeated by Titus Quinctius – did not have much of a state compared to the great power of the Romans and Greeks who attacked him; none the less, because he was a good soldier and knew how to hold the people and to secure himself from the nobility, he was able to wage war against them for many years; and if at the end he lost possession of several cities, he was nevertheless left with his kingdom.

Therefore, these princes of ours who have been in their principalities for many years, and who have then lost them, must not blame fortune but rather their own idleness; for, never having thought in peaceful times that things might change (which is a common defect in men, not to consider in good weather the possibility of a tempest), when adverse times finally arrived they thought about running away and not about defending themselves; and they hoped that the people, angered by the insolence of the victors, would eventually recall them. This policy, when others are lacking, is good; but it is indeed bad to have disregarded all other solutions for this one; for you should never wish to fall, believing that you will find someone else to pick you up; because whether this occurs or not, it does not increase your security, that method being a cowardly defence and one not dependent upon your own resources. And those methods alone are good, are certain, are lasting, that depend on yourself and your own ingenuity.

CHAPTER XXV

On Fortune's Role in Human Affairs and How She Can Be Dealt With

IT is not unknown to me that many have held, and still hold, the opinion that the things of this world are, in a manner, controlled by fortune and by God, that men with their wisdom cannot control them, and, on the contrary, that men can have no remedy whatsoever for them; and for this reason they might judge that they need not sweat much over such matters but let them be governed by fate. This opinion has been more strongly held in our own times because of the great variation of affairs that has been observed and that is being observed every day which is beyond human conjecture. Sometimes, as I think about these things, I am inclined to their opinion to a certain extent. Nevertheless, in order that our free will be not extinguished, I judge it to be true that fortune is the arbiter of one half of our actions,* but that she still leaves the control of the other half, or almost that, to us. And I compare her to one of those ruinous rivers that, when they become enraged, flood the plains, tear down the trees and buildings, taking up earth from one spot and placing it upon another; everyone flees from them, everyone yields to their onslaught, unable to oppose them in any way. But although they are of such a nature, it does not follow that when the weather is calm we cannot take precautions with embankments and dikes, so that when they rise up again either the waters will be channelled off or their impetus will not be either so unchecked or so damaging. The same things happen where fortune is concerned: she shows her force where there is no organized strength to resist her; and she directs her impact there where she knows that dikes and embankments are not constructed to hold her. And if you consider Italy, the seat of these changes and the nation which has set them in motion, you will see a country without embankments and without a single bastion: for if she were defended by the necessary forces, like Germany, Spain, and France, either this flood would not have produced the great changes that it has or it would not have come upon us at all. And this I consider enough to say about fortune in general terms.

But, limiting myself more to particulars, I say that one sees a prince prosper today and come to ruin tomorrow without having seen him change his character or any of the reasons that have been discussed at length earlier; that is, that a prince who relies completely upon fortune will come to ruin as soon as she changes; I also believe that the man who adapts his course of action to the nature of the times will succeed and, likewise, that the man who sets his course of action out of tune with the times will come to grief. For one can observe that men, in the affairs which lead them to the end that they seek – that is, glory and wealth – proceed in different ways; one by caution, another with impetuousness; one through violence, another with guile; one with patience, another with its opposite; and each one by these various means can attain his goals. And we also see, in the case of two cautious men, that one reaches his goal while the other does not; and, likewise, two men equally succeed using two different means, one being cautious and the other impetuous: this arises from nothing else than the nature of the times that either suit or do not suit their course of action. From this results that which I have said, that two men, working in opposite ways, can produce the same outcome; and of two men working in the same fashion one achieves his goal and the other does not. On this also depends the variation of what is good; for, if a man governs himself with caution and patience, and the times and conditions are turning in such a way that his policy is a good one, he will prosper; but if the times and conditions change, he will be ruined because he does not change his method of procedure. Nor is there to be found a man so prudent that he knows how to adapt himself to this, both because he cannot deviate from that to which he is by nature inclined and also because he cannot be persuaded to depart from a path, having always prospered by following it. And therefore the cautious man, when it is time to act impetuously, does not know how to do so, and he is ruined; but if he had changed his conduct with the times, fortune would not have changed.

Pope Julius II acted impetuously in all his affairs, and he found the times and conditions so apt to this course of action that he always achieved successful results. Consider the first campaign he waged against Bologna while Messer Giovanni Bentivogli was still alive. The Venetians were unhappy about it; so was the King of Spain; Julius still had negotiations going on about it with France; and nevertheless, he started personally on this expedition with his usual ferocity and lack of caution. Such a move kept Spain and the Venetians at bay, the latter out of fear and the former out of a desire to regain the entire Kingdom of Naples; and at the same time it drew the King of France into the affair, for when the King saw that the Pope had already made this move, he judged that he could not deny him the use of his troops without obviously harming him, since he wanted his friendship in order to defeat the Venetians. And therefore Julius achieved with his impetuous action what no other pontiff would ever have achieved with the greatest of human wisdom; for, if he had waited to leave Rome with agreements settled and things in order, as any other pontiff might have done, he would never have succeeded, because the King of France would have found a thousand excuses and the others would have aroused in him a thousand fears. I wish to leave unmentioned his other deeds, which were all similar and which were all successful. And the brevity of his life* did not let him experience the opposite, since if times which necessitated caution had come his ruin would have followed from it: for never would he have deviated from those methods to which his nature inclined him.

I conclude, therefore, that since fortune changes and men remain set in their ways, men will succeed when the two are in harmony and fail when they are not in accord. I am certainly convinced of this: that it is better to be impetuous than cautious, because fortune is a woman,* and it is necessary, in order to keep her down, to beat her and to struggle with her. And it is seen that she more often allows herself to be taken over by men who are impetuous than by those who make cold advances; and then, being a woman, she is always the friend of young men, for they are less cautious, more aggressive, and they command her with more audacity.

CHAPTER XXVI

An Exhortation to Liberate Italy From the Barbarians

CONSIDERING, therefore, all of the things mentioned above, and reflecting as to whether the times are suitable, at present, to honour a new prince in Italy, and if there is the material that might give a skilful and prudent prince the opportunity to introduce a form of government that would bring him honour and good to the people of Italy, it seems to me that so many circumstances are favourable to such a new prince that I know of no other time more appropriate. And if, as I said, it was necessary that the people of Israel be slaves in Egypt in order to recognize Moses' ability, and it was necessary that the Persians be oppressed by the Medes to recognize the greatness of spirit in Cyrus, and it was necessary that the Athenians be dispersed to realize the excellence of Theseus, then, likewise, at the present time, in order to recognize the ability of an Italian spirit, it was necessary that Italy be reduced to her present condition and that she be more enslaved than the Hebrews, more servile than the Persians, more scattered than the Athenians; without a leader, without organization, beaten, despoiled, ripped apart, overrun, and prey to every sort of catastrophe.

And even though before now some glimmer of light may have shown itself in a single individual,* so that it was possible to believe that God had ordained him for Italy's redemption, nevertheless it was witnessed afterwards how at the height of his career he was rejected by fortune. So now Italy remains without life and awaits the man who can heal her wounds and put an end to the plundering of Lombardy, the ransoms in the Kingdom of Naples and in Tuscany, and who can cure her of those sores which have been festering for so long. Look how she now prays to God to send someone to redeem her from these barbaric cruelties and insolence; see her still ready and willing to follow a banner, provided that there be someone to raise it up. Nor is there anyone in sight, at present, in whom she can have more hope than in your illustrious house,* which, with its fortune and ability, favoured by God and by the Church, of which it is now prince, could make itself the head of this redemption. This will not be very difficult if you keep before you the deeds and the lives of those named above. And although those men were out of the ordinary and marvellous, they were nevertheless men; and each of them had less opportunity than the present one; for their enterprises were no more just, nor easier, nor was God more a friend to them than to you. Here justice is great: 'Only those wars that are necessary are just, and arms are sacred when there is no hope except through arms.'* Here there is a great willingness; and where there is a great willingness there cannot be great difficulty, if only you will use the institutions of those men I have proposed as your target. Besides this, we now see extraordinary, unprecedented signs brought about by God: the sea has opened up; a cloud has shown you the path; the rock pours forth water; it has rained manna here; everything has converged for your greatness. The rest you must do yourself. God does not wish to do everything, in order not to take from us our free will and that part of the glory which is ours.

And it is no surprise if some of the Italians mentioned previously were not capable of doing what it is hoped may be done by your illustrious house, and if, during the many revolutions in Italy and the many campaigns of war, it always seems that her military ability is spent. This results from the fact that her ancient institutions were not good and that there was no one who knew how to discover new ones; and no other thing brings a new man on the rise such honour as the new laws and the new institutions discovered by him. These things, when they are well founded and have in themselves a certain greatness, make him revered and admirable. And in Italy there is no lack of material to be given a form: here there is great ability in her members, were it not for the lack of it in her leaders. Consider how in duels and skirmishes involving just a few men the Italians are superior in strength, dexterity, and cunning; but when it comes to armies they do not match others. And all this comes from the weakness of her leaders; for those who know are not followed; and with each one seeming to know, there has not been to the present day anyone who has known how to set himself above the others, either because of ingenuity or fortune, so that others might yield to him. As a consequence, during so much time, during the many wars fought over the past twenty years, whenever there has been an army made up completely of Italians it has always made a poor showing. As proof of this, there is first Taro, then Alexandria, Capua, Genoa, Vailà, Bologna, and Mestri.*

Therefore, if your illustrious house desires to follow these excellent men who redeemed their lands, it is necessary before all else, as a true basis for every undertaking, to provide yourself with your own native troops, for one cannot have either more faithful, more loyal, or better troops. And although each one separately may be brave, all of them united will become even braver when they find themselves commanded, honoured, and well treated by their own prince. It is necessary, therefore, to prepare yourself with such troops as these, so that with Italian strength you will be able to defend yourself from foreigners. And although Swiss and Spanish infantry may be reputed terrifying, nevertheless both have defects, so that a third army could not only oppose them but be confident of defeating them. For the Spanish cannot withstand cavalry and the Swiss have a fear of foot soldiers they meet in combat who are as brave as they are. Therefore, it has been witnessed and experience will demonstrate that the Spanish cannot withstand French cavalry and the Swiss are ruined by Spanish infantry-men. And although this last point has not been completely confirmed by experience, there was nevertheless a hint of it at the battle of Ravenna,* when the Spanish infantry met the German battalions, who follow the same order as the Swiss; and the Spanish, with their agile bodies, aided by their spiked shields, entered between and underneath the Germans' long pikes and were safe, without the Germans having any recourse against them; and had it not been for the cavalry charge that broke them, the Spaniards would have slaughtered them all. Therefore, as the defects of both these kinds of troops are recognized, a new type can be instituted which can stand up to cavalry and will have no fear of foot soldiers: this will come about by creating new armies and changing battle formations. And these are among those matters that, when newly organized, give reputation and greatness to a new prince.

This opportunity, therefore, must not be permitted to pass by so that Italy, after so long a time, may behold its redeemer. Nor can I express with what love he will be received in all those provinces that have suffered through these foreign floods; with what thirst for revenge, with what obstinate loyalty, with what compassion, with what tears! What doors will be closed to him? Which people will deny him obedience? What jealousy could oppose him? What Italian would deny him homage? For everyone, this barbarian dominion stinks! Therefore, may your illustrious house take up this mission with that spirit and with that hope in which just undertakings are begun; so that under your banner this country may be ennobled and, under your guidance, those words of Petrarch may come true:

> Ingenuity over rage
> Will take up arms; and the battle will be short.
> For ancient valour
> In Italian hearts is not yet dead.*

EXPLANATORY NOTES

DEDICATORY PREFACE

5 *Lorenzo de' Medici, the Magnificent*: this figure, the Duke of Urbino (1492–1519) should not be confused with his more illustrious grandfather, Lorenzo il Magnifico (1449–92). Lorenzo received Machiavelli's dedication after an earlier preface to *The Prince* originally intended for Giuliano de' Medici, Duke of Nemours (1479–1516) had to be changed when Giuliano suddenly died. Neither of these Medici princelings ever measured up to Machiavelli's estimation of their potential, and it is ironic that they are remembered today by Michelangelo's magnificent sculptures of them for the Medici Chapel at San Lorenzo in Florence. While the bulk of *The Prince* was completed in 1513, this dedication was probably composed between 1516 and 1519 after Lorenzo was named Duke of Urbino by Pope Leo X (1516) but before his subsequent death (1519).

CHAPTER I

7 *Francesco Sforza*: the famous mercenary soldier (1401–66) who married the daughter of Filippo Maria Visconti, Duke of Milan, and eventually became that city's ruler in 1450.

King of Spain: Ferdinand II of Aragon (1452–1516) agreed to divide the Kingdom of Naples with Louis XII of France in the Treaty of Granada (11 November 1500); however, the two monarchs soon disagreed over the division of the spoils, and after a number of military defeats, the French recognized Ferdinand as King of Naples in the Treaty of Blois (12 October 1505).

CHAPTER II

republics...elsewhere at length: while this remark has caused a great deal of debate and has led some scholars to claim that Machiavelli's *Discourses* were begun before *The Prince* (since Book I of that work deals at length with the subject), it is most likely that this sentence was added to *The Prince* after it was finished, while Machiavelli was writing *The Discourses*.

8 *Duke of Ferrara*: Machiavelli here compresses together events from the lives of two different rulers of Ferrara: Ercole d'Este (1471–1505), who lost a good deal of territory to Venice and her ally, Pope Sixtus IV, in a war he fought with King Ferrante of Naples; and his son Alfonso d'Este (1486–1534), who was attacked by Pope Julius II when the Pope formed the Holy League against France in 1510.

Pope Julius: Giuliano della Rovere (1443–1513, made Pope in 1503), an energetic leader, diplomat, and soldier whose various achievements included the strengthening of the Papal States in Central Italy and the organization of the League of Cambrai against Venice and the Holy League against France. Julius II was also the patron of Michelangelo, Raphael, and Bramante.

space for the construction of another: here Machiavelli employs a technical term, *addentellato*, referring to a tooth-like series of stones on a building or at the end of a wall left to assist the builder in continuing the structure.

CHAPTER III

strong measures: literally, *medicine forti* or 'strong medicines'.

Louis XII, King of France: the son of Charles d'Orléans (1462–1515), he succeeded his cousin Charles VIII to the throne in 1498 and pursued hereditary claims to both Naples and Milan; allied with the Venetians, he occupied Milan briefly in 1499 but lost it to the Duke of Milan in 1500 after a rebellion against the French governor of the city.

9 *Ludovico*: Ludovico Sforza (1451–1508), called 'il Moro' ('The Moor'), and son of Francesco Sforza, Duke of Milan, and Bianca Maria Visconti, who married Beatrice d'Este and became Duke of Milan in 1494 after the French invasion of Italy and the death of his nephew, Gian Galeazzo Visconti (whom he may have murdered). While Ludovico managed to retake Milan in 1500, in that same year his army confronted the French at Novara, and when Ludovico's Swiss mercenaries refused to do battle with their fellow countrymen in Louis' service, Sforza was captured and spent the rest of his life in prison near Tours. He was one of Leonardo da Vinci's patrons.

the whole world: France held Milan until shortly after the battle of Ravenna (1512), a Pyrrhic victory in which French troops were victorious against the Holy League led by Pope Julius II but lost their gallant commander-in-chief, Gaston de Foix. Machiavelli's remark that the 'whole world' opposed France refers to the fact that the Holy League included not only Spain, Venice, and the Pope, but – at least on paper – Henry VIII of England and the German Emperor, Maximilian I.

Burgundy...Normandy: Normandy was annexed to France in 1204, and Gascony was taken back from the English in 1453; Burgundy was joined to France in 1477, while Brittany was acquired in 1491 through the marriage of Charles VIII and Anne of Brittany, who subsequently married Louis XII.

11 *the Aetolians brought the Romans into Greece*: in 211 BC the Aetolian League, an alliance of federated states in Greece, allied itself to Rome against Philip V of Macedonia (220–178 BC). It opposed the Achaean League, composed of other Greek states allied to Macedonia.

12 *the Macedonian kingdom was put down*: Philip V of Macedonia was defeated at the battle of Cynoscephalae (197 BC), giving Rome control of Greece.

Antiochus was driven out: Antiochus (223–187 BC), King of Syria, invaded Greece and was finally defeated by the Romans at the battle of Magnesia (190 BC).

what physicians say about disease: the specific disease Machiavelli has in mind here is consumption or tuberculosis.

13 *and not of Charles*: Charles VIII (1470–98) invaded Italy in 1494 to assert his hereditary claim to the Kingdom of Naples; after taking Naples in 1495, he was opposed by the League of Venice – Milan, Venice, Spain, Pope Alexander VI, and the Emperor – and withdrew from Italy safely after escaping entrapment by a superior Italian force at the battle of Fornovo (1495). His cousin Louis, Duke of Orléans, succeeded him as Louis XII.

Genoa surrendered...all rushed to gain his friendship: after Louis XII took Milan in 1499, Genoa surrendered; the Florentines became his allies in return for assistance in their campaign to conquer Pisa in the same year; the rulers Machiavelli mentions in the various city-states or duchies in this passage include Francesco Gonzaga (Mantua), Ercole d'Este (Ferrara), Giovanni Bentivogli and his son Annibale (Bologna), Caterina Sforza Riario (Forlì), Astorre Manfredi (Faenza), Giovanni

Sforza (Pesaro), Pandolfo Malatesta (Rimini), Giulio Cesare da Varano (Camerino), and Jacopo d'Appiano (Piombino).

15 *the annulment of his marriage and for the Cardinal's hat of Rouen*: in return for a dispensation allowing Louis XII to divorce his wife, Joanne, and to marry Anne of Brittany, widow of Charles VIII, as well as the promotion of his favourite, Georges d'Amboise, then Archbishop of Rouen, to the rank of Cardinal, the King agreed to assist Pope Alexander VI in regaining parts of the Romagna for the Papal States.

And I spoke about this at Nantes: Machiavelli was in France on a diplomatic mission for the Florentine Republic in 1500 and on several other occasions.

Cesare Borgia, son of Pope Alexander: born in 1476, the son of the then Cardinal Rodrigo Borgia and Vanozza Catanei, Cesare became a Cardinal in 1493; he renounced a promising career in the Church in 1498, and was made a Duke by Louis XII, receiving promise of French support in the conquest of the Romagna. When the reign of his father (1492–1503) ended unexpectedly, Cesare's power evaporated, and he died in Spain in 1507.

CHAPTER IV

16 *Alexander the Great*: ruler of Macedonia (356–323 BC) and conqueror of the last Persian ruler, Darius III (336–331 BC).

18 *Pyrrhus*: King of Epirus (319–272 BC), who waged war on the Romans in Italy and from whose military campaigns derives the phrase 'Pyrrhic victory'.

CHAPTER V

19 *just as Pisa did*: after obtaining Pisa from the Visconti family in 1405 and capturing the city in the following year, Florence controlled this important seaport until 1494, then regained it after numerous sieges in 1509.

CHAPTER VI

20 *prudent archers*: it is interesting that Baldesar Castiglione, author of *The Book of the Courtier* (1528), the only other Italian book to rival Machiavelli's *Prince* in popularity during the

European Renaissance, employs this same metaphor to describe his concept of imitation.

either ingenuity or fortune: Chapter VI contains numerous references to the special Machiavellian quality of *virtù*, translated variously in this edition according to the context of Machiavelli's argument as 'skill', 'ingenuity', 'ability', but rarely 'virtue' in the moral sense of the English word. It is impossible to render this complex term by any single English word, for Machiavelli himself did not employ the Italian word in a strictly technical sense with only a single, well-defined meaning.

Moses, Cyrus, Romulus, Theseus, and the like: only Cyrus, founder of the Persian Empire (599–529 BC) is a purely political figure, although Machiavelli's knowledge of his life probably came from Xenophon's idealized view in his *Cyropaedia*. According to Biblical narrative, Moses instituted the laws of the Israelites (although they were given to him by God); Romulus was the mythical founder of Rome in 753 BC, just as Theseus was the legendary King of Athens. It is noteworthy that Machiavelli, supposedly a hard-boiled realist, employs literary or mythical figures as his ideal model for the new prince.

22 *Brother Girolamo Savonarola*: a Dominican preacher born in Ferrara in 1452, Savonarola became Prior of San Marco in Florence in 1491, and was a major force in Florentine politics after the expulsion of the Medici in 1494. A fierce republican, Savonarola lost favour in the city after Pope Alexander VI excommunicated him, and in 1498 he was executed in the Piazza della Signoria. He was the author of an important political work, *Treatise on the Organization and Government of Florence* (1498), which proposed a republican government for the city and an enlarged grand council based on his interpretation of that branch of the Venetian government.

Hiero of Syracuse: Commander of the army of Syracuse, Hiero II (*c.*306–215 BC) seized power and ruled the city as its tyrant; after an initial alliance with Carthage during the early days of the First Punic War, he made peace with Rome and remained her ally.

CHAPTER VII

24 *and when this no longer existed, he lost it*: the sudden death of Alexander VI occurred in August of 1503.

Orsini, Colonnesi, and their allies: the Orsini and Colonna families, both powerful Roman clans, were traditional enemies, but neither group could be trusted by Cesare Borgia or Pope Alexander in their quest for power.

26 *and into his hands*: Borgia's treachery at Sinigaglia (31 December 1502) led to the strangulation of his adversaries – Oliverotto Euffreducci (ruler of Fermo) and Vitellozzo Vitelli were killed immediately; Paulo Francesco Orsini died a few days later.

Messer Remirro de Orco: named governor of the Romagna in 1501, Cesare Borgia's lieutenant was removed in order to win favour from the fickle populace of the area.

28 *by the brevity of Alexander's life*: here Machiavelli refers to the comparative brevity of Alexander's pontificate (eleven years), not to his age when he died. In Chapter XI, Machiavelli remarks that the average length of a pontificate was about ten years.

29 *San Pietro ad Vincula, Colonna, San Giorgio, Ascanio*: these four Cardinals are Giuliano della Rovere (later Pope Julius II), called 'St Peter's in Chains' by Machiavelli, who follows the common practice of designating a Cardinal by the church to which his office was attached; Giovanni Colonna (d. 1508); Raffaello Riario, Cardinal of San Giorgio (d. 1521); and Ascanio Sforza, son of Francesco Sforza.

the election of Rouen: Georges d'Amboise, Cardinal of Rouen, whom Machiavelli believes Cesare Borgia should have supported for the papacy through pressure upon Spanish and French prelates.

CHAPTER VIII

30 *Agathocles the Sicilian*: tyrant of Syracuse (361–289 BC).

it cannot be called ingenuity: readers of *The Prince* who insist upon interpreting Machiavelli as an immoral or amoral counsellor of evil should not overlook this passage, in which Machiavellian *virtù* (skill, ability, ingenuity) is clearly distinguished from naked power. In other words, only a few very specific ends could ever justify such drastic means for Machiavelli.

CHAPTER IX

35 *Nabis*: tyrant of Sparta after 207 BC, who was attacked by Rome and most of Greece in 195 BC during the Second Macedonian War.

the Gracchi of Rome: popular Roman reformers and tribunes, Tiberius Sempronius Gracchus (d. 133 BC) and his brother Gaius Sempronius Gracchus (d. 121 BC), both met their deaths as a result of their efforts on behalf of the Roman lower classes.

36 *Messer Giorgio Scali*: a wealthy Florentine who became head of the popular faction after the Ciompi Revolt of 1378; Scali was beheaded in 1382 after he led an attack upon the palace of one of the city's magistrates.

CHAPTER X

37 *The first case...on the subject*: see Chapter VI for Machiavelli's earlier discussion, as well as Chapters XII and XIII for his later remarks.

I detailed above (and discuss below): see Chapters IX and XIX for these discussions.

CHAPTER XI

40 *Pope Sixtus*: Francesco della Rovere, Pope Sixtus IV (1471–84), the uncle of Giuliano della Rovere, later Pope Julius II.

Then came Pope Julius: Giuliano della Rovere ruled as Julius II from 1503 until 1513.

41 *His Holiness Pope Leo*: Cardinal Giovanni de' Medici succeeded Pope Julius II in March 1513 and reigned as pontiff with the title Leo X until 1521.

CHAPTER XII

42 *a piece of chalk*: this expression refers to the practice Charles VIII followed in marking the homes to be used for quartering his troops during the invasion of Italy in 1494–5; the contemptuous tone of Machiavelli's remark underscores his belief that Italian resistance was virtually non-existent. This remark is attributed to Pope Alexander VI by the French historian Philippe de Commynes (*Mémoires* VII, 14).

And the man...spoke the truth: most probably, this is a reference to Girolamo Savonarola, whose sermon of 1 November 1494 interpreted the Italian invasion by Charles VIII as a punishment for the sins of Italy, Florence, and the Church.

43 *Philip of Macedonia*: King of Macedonia (359–336 BC) and father of Alexander the Great. Philip was not, strictly speaking, a mercenary.

Epaminondas: Theban general (d. 362 BC) who defected Sparta at the Battle of Leuctra (371 BC).

Queen Giovanna of Naples: ruler of Naples (1414–35), who hired mercenaries (Sforza and others) to defend her kingdom.

John Hawkwood: an English knight who came to Italy in 1361 and served Florence as a mercenary until his death in 1393 (known in Italy as Giovanni Acuto).

the Bracceschi: mercenary troops commanded by Braccio da Montone (1368–1424) who opposed other mercenaries under Sforza in the service of Queen Giovanna of Naples.

Paulo Vitelli: Florentine mercenary executed by his employers in 1499 after an unsatisfactory performance at the Siege of Pisa, and the brother of Vitellozzo Vitelli, strangled by Cesare Borgia at Sinigaglia.

44 *Carmagnola*: Francesco Bussone, Count of Carmagnola (c. 1380–1432), a Venetian soldier of fortune executed by Venice for suspected double-dealing with his Visconti opponents.

Bartolomeo da Bergamo...the Count of Pitigliano: Bartolomeo Colleoni (1400–75) fought in the service of Venice and is remembered by the magnificent equestrian statue Verrocchio erected in the city; Roberto da San Severino commanded Venetian troops in a war with Ferrara (1482–4); Niccolò Orsini, Count of Pitigliano (1442–1510), was the Venetian commander at the disastrous battle of Vailà against the forces of Pope Julius II.

as occurred later at Vailà: at the battle of Vailà or Agnadello in 1509, the Venetians were defeated by French troops.

45 *Alberigo of Conio*: Alberigo da Barbiano (d. 1409) was the founder of a famous company of mercenaries composed entirely of Italian rather than foreign troops.

CHAPTER XIII

46 *The emperor of Constantinople*: the Byzantine ruler, John VI, Cantacuzenus (*c.* 1292–1383).

47 *an example from the Old Testament*: the figure of David played an important role in Florentine republican iconography, as is clear from the fact that the famous statues of David by Donatello, Verrocchio, and Michelangelo all once stood near the Palazzo della Signoria, the seat of government. Machiavelli takes the story of David and Saul from 1 Sam. 17.

48 *as I said earlier*: see Chapter III.

49 '*nothing is so unhealthy...one's own power*': Machiavelli here cites from the original Latin of Tacitus (*Annals* XIII, 19), probably from memory.

CHAPTER XIV

as will be treated below: see Chapters XV and XIX.

50 *Philopoemen*: Greek general (253–182 BC) and head of the Achaean League; his speech is taken from accounts in Plutarch's *Parallel Lives* and Livy (XXXV, 28).

51 *Scipio*: Publius Cornelius Scipio Africanus (236–184 BC), the victor over Hannibal and Carthage in the Second Punic War.

the life of Cyrus: Xenophon (*c.* 430–*c.* 354 BC) wrote an idealized biography of Cyrus, the *Cyropaedia*, much admired during Machiavelli's day.

CHAPTER XV

52 *the effectual truth...rather than its imagined one*: Machiavelli has in mind here not only Plato but also the many abstract portraits of idealized rulers or Christian princes composed by the Latin humanists.

CHAPTER XVII

55 *the destruction of Pistoia*: when violent squabbles broke out between the Cancellieri and the Panciatichi factions of this Florentine subject-city in 1501–2, Machiavelli was sent there several times in an attempt to restore order.

'*My difficult condition...on all sides*': Machiavelli cites the original Latin from Virgil's *Aeneid* (I, 563–4).

56 *as I said earlier*: see Chapter IX.

57 *Hannibal*: Commander of the Carthaginian army (249–183 BC) who was defeated by Scipio at the Battle of Zama in 202 BC, ending the Second Punic War.

Fabius Maximus: Roman consul and dictator in 217 BC (d. 203 BC), whose delaying tactics against Hannibal while his army was ravaging Italy were opposed by Scipio, who wished to wage a more aggressive offensive campaign.

CHAPTER XVIII

58 *two means of fighting*: Machiavelli takes this argument from Cicero, *De officiis* (I, xi), but changes it quite drastically.

Chiron the Centaur: Machiavelli's strange allegorical interpretation of Chiron's dual nature has no apparent classical source and was probably a product of his own fantasy.

the fox and the lion: Machiavelli found this soon-to-become famous idea in Cicero's *De officiis* (I, xiii), but he changes Cicero's argument completely. Cicero had maintained that both force and treachery were inhuman and, therefore, contemptible policies.

60 *one must consider the final result*: the Italian original, *si guarda al fine*, has often been misconstrued to imply that Machiavelli meant 'the end justifies the means', something he never said in *The Prince*. For another important statement concerning ends and means, see Machiavelli's discussion of Romulus in *The Discourses* (I, ix).

a certain prince of the present day: probably Ferdinand II of Aragon.

CHAPTER XIX

62 *Messer Annibale Bentivogli*: Annibale Bentivogli was murdered by rivals in 1445; his son Giovanni took power in Bologna in 1462, and after his death in 1508 Giovanni was succeeded by his son, 'the present Messer Annibale' (1469–1540).

64 *all those emperors...and Maximinus*: Machiavelli refers to the succession of Roman rulers between AD 161 and AD 238: the philosopher-soldier Marcus Aurelius (121–80); his son Commodus (180–93); Pertinax (193); Julian (193); Severus (193–211);

his son Caracalla (211–17); Macrinus (217–18); Heliogabalus (218–22); Alexander (222–35); and Maximinus (235–38). Machiavelli's source for his discussion of these men is most likely the Latin translation of Herodian's Greek history done by Angelo Poliziano and first published in 1493.

68 *except the Turk and the Sultan*: the ruler of Turkey at this time was the Ottoman Selim I; the Sultan is that of Mamluk Egypt, who was selected from among the commanders of the slave army. Selim I overthrew the Mamluks' power in 1517.

CHAPTER XX

71 *the Guelf and Ghibelline factions*: in the struggle between Emperor and Pope during the Middle Ages in Italy, Guelfs supported the papacy, while Ghibellines favoured the Emperor. International rivalries, however, were mixed with local squabbles, and one faction would turn to assistance from the Pope if its rivals received aid from the Emperor, and vice versa.

Pandolfo Petrucci: ruler of Siena from the end of the Quattrocento until his death in 1512. Machiavelli visited his court several times on diplomatic missions.

72 *Messer Niccolò Vitelli*: driven out of Città di Castello by Pope Sixtus IV in 1474, Vitelli returned to power in 1482 with Florentine assistance and destroyed two fortresses the Pope had built.

Guido Ubaldo: Guidobaldo da Montefeltro, Duke of Urbino (1472–1508), was driven out of Urbino in 1502 by Cesare Borgia but returned there briefly during the same year to destroy some of the city's fortifications; his court inspired Castiglione's *Book of the Courtier* (1528).

the Bentivolgi: driven from Bologna in 1506 by Pope Julius II, the family returned in 1511.

73 *the Countess of Forlì*: Caterina Sforza Riario, niece of Ludovico Sforza Il Moro, took refuge in the Forlì fortress when her husband Girolamo was assassinated in 1498 until her uncle sent help; Cesare Borgia captured Forlì as well as Imola from her in 1500.

CHAPTER XXI

74 *Messer Bernabò Visconti*: ruler of Milan from 1354 until 1385 and infamous for his ingeniously cruel punishments.

CHAPTER XXII

77 *Messer Antonio da Venafro*: Antonio Giordani from Venafro (b. 1459) was one of Petrucci's most trusted advisers.

CHAPTER XXIII

79 *Father Luca*: Machiavelli encountered Luca Rainaldi, one of the chief ministers of Emperor Maximilian I (1459–1519), during one of his diplomatic missions abroad.

CHAPTER XXIV

80 *Philip of Macedonia*: Philip V of Macedonia (221–179 BC), defeated at the battle of Cynoscephalae (197 BC).

CHAPTER XXV

82 *fortune is the arbiter of one half of our actions*: Machiavelli's conception of the 'new prince', his *virtù*, and the important opportunities chance might provide him to achieve power, all presuppose a certain amount of human freedom. His discussion of fortune, however, owes more to his poetic inclinations than to a dispassionate philosophical discussion of the weighty issues involved in the conflict between human free will and determinism.

84 *And the brevity of his life*: once again, as he had earlier done in discussing Pope Alexander VI (Chapter VII), Machiavelli is referring to the brevity of the pontificate of Julius II, not to the brevity of the man's life itself.

Fortune is a woman: here, Machiavelli clearly draws a parallel between the energy required for a violent sexual encounter and that which determines the drive for political power.

CHAPTER XXVI

85 *a single individual*: this is probably a reference to Cesare Borgia, but Machiavelli may also be referring to Giuliano de' Medici, Duke of Nemours, whose sudden death in 1516 forced Machiavelli to change the dedication of *The Prince*.

your illustrious house: by 1516, the probable date of the dedication of *The Prince*, Medici family members occupied the papacy (Leo X), and Lorenzo de' Medici, appointed Duke of Urbino by Leo in that year, was obviously intended to be the future ruler of Florence. When Machiavelli wrote *The Prince* in 1513, he first envisioned a convergence of Medici power in Giuliano de' Medici, Duke of Nemours, and Pope Leo; after Giuliano's death in 1516, this possibility was kept alive with the brief appearance of Lorenzo de' Medici. This opportunity paralleled the opportunity that existed with a Borgia Pope, Alexander VI, and his son Cesare, until the Pope died suddenly in 1503. With the deaths of both Giuliano and Lorenzo by 1519, Medici hopes faded away, and this probably explains why Machiavelli never bothered to publish *The Prince* before his death, since the practical purpose of the little book no longer existed after 1519.

'*Only those wars . . . except through arms*': cited by Machiavelli from the original Latin of Livy (IX, i).

86 *first Taro . . . and Mestri:* a list of Italian military defeats in chronological order for rhetorical effect: Charles VIII was victorious over Italian forces at Fornovo (1495) near the Taro River; Louis XII took Alexandria (1499), Capua (1501), Genoa (1507), Valià (1509), and Bologna (1511); the Venetians were defeated near Vicenza in 1513 by foreign troops, resulting in the sack of Mestri (modern Mestre).

87 *the battle of Ravenna*: on 11 April 1512, the French cavalry under Gaston de Foix routed Spanish infantrymen.

88 *Ingenuity over rage . . . is not yet dead*: lines from Petrarch's canzone, 'Italia mia' (ll. 93–6). In citing from Petrarch's patriotic poem, Machiavelli focuses our attention on Petrarch's opposition of *virtù* and *furore* and asserts that his own *virtù* (ingenuity, a disciplined strength) will eventually triumph over undisciplined anger in the creation of an Italian state by the Medici prince.

THE WORLD'S CLASSICS

A Select List

JANE AUSTEN: Emma
Edited by James Kinsley and David Lodge

WILLIAM BECKFORD: Vathek
Edited by Roger Lonsdale

JOHN BUNYAN: The Pilgrim's Progress
Edited by N. H. Keeble

THOMAS CARLYLE: The French Revolution
Edited by K. J. Fielding and David Sorensen

GEOFFREY CHAUCER: The Canterbury Tales
Translated by David Wright

CHARLES DICKENS: Christmas Books
Edited by Ruth Glancy

BENJAMIN DISRAELI: Coningsby
Edited by Sheila M. Smith

MARIA EDGEWORTH: Castle Rackrent
Edited by George Watson

SUSAN FERRIER: Marriage
Edited by Herbert Foltinek

ELIZABETH GASKELL: Cousin Phillis and Other Tales
Edited by Angus Easson

THOMAS HARDY: A Pair of Blue Eyes
Edited by Alan Manford

HOMER: The Iliad
Translated by Robert Fitzgerald
Introduction by G. S. Kirk

HENRIK IBSEN: An Enemy of the People, The Wild Duck,
Rosmersholm
Edited and Translated by James McFarlane

HENRY JAMES: The Ambassadors
Edited by Christopher Butler

JOCELIN OF BRAKELOND:
Chronicle of the Abbey of Bury St. Edmunds
Translated by Diana Greenway and Jane Sayers

BEN JONSON: Five Plays
Edited by G. A. Wilkes

LEONARDO DA VINCI: Notebooks
Edited by Irma A. Richter

HERMAN MELVILLE: The Confidence-Man
Edited by Tony Tanner

PROSPER MÉRIMÉE: Carmen and Other Stories
Translated by Nicholas Jotcham

EDGAR ALLAN POE: Selected Tales
Edited by Julian Symons

MARY SHELLEY: Frankenstein
Edited by M. K. Joseph

BRAM STOKER: Dracula
Edited by A. N. Wilson

ANTHONY TROLLOPE: The American Senator
Edited by John Halperin

OSCAR WILDE: Complete Shorter Fiction
Edited by Isobel Murray